The Confederate Quartermaster
in the
Trans-Mississippi

The Confederate Quartermaster
in the
Trans-Mississippi

by

James L. Nichols

UNIVERSITY OF TEXAS PRESS · AUSTIN

Preface and Acknowledgments

About twenty-five years ago Professor Charles W. Ramsdell, in his presidential address to the Southern Historical Association, wondered why the military historians had neglected the story of the Confederate Army supply services.[1] In the same vein the eminent biographer and historian Douglas Southall Freeman called attention to the need for such studies of supply in his significant book *The South to Posterity*.[2] In recent years the gaps have been closing with the appearance of an increasing number of studies of the ordnance and railroad problems of the embattled South. To date, however, the equally vital subsistence and quartermaster departments have failed to inspire full-length treatments. The bleak prospect of wading through scattered masses of receipts, memoranda, and account books quickly blunts the enthusiasm of many Confederate monographers. Truly it may be said that in this realm of bookkeeping bureaus one will not want for elbow room.

My interest in this subject derives from several obvious stimuli. In 1946, while I was seeking a suitable subject for my Master's thesis, Professor Barnes F. Lathrop of The University of Texas and Professor Frank E. Vandiver of Rice University (who was then at Texas on a Rockefeller Foundation grant) suggested the possibilities of a study of Trans-Mississippi quartermaster supply. The University of Texas had recently acquired a fine set of manuscripts, the Heartman Collection, among which were films of the fairly complete papers of Captain N. A. Birge, who served as combat unit quartermaster, as post quartermaster at the important depots of Monroe and Shreveport, Louisiana, and finally as a principal purchasing and transportation quartermaster for the Cotton Bureau of the Trans-Mississippi Department. Because I had just completed three years of service as supply officer of the 146th Engineer Combat Battalion, it seemed appropriate for me to see what kind of story could be drawn from the well-kept files of Captain Birge.

[1] Charles W. Ramsdell, "Some Problems Involved in Writing the History of the Confederacy," *Journal of Southern History*, II (May, 1936), 137.
[2] Douglas Southall Freeman, *The South to Posterity*, p. 199.

Anyone who has ever been saddled with military supply responsibility, a twenty-five-hour job, will not wonder at my built-in sympathy for these supply men. Supply people in any army seldom escape being targets for the complaints of nonsupply personnel, even when things are going well for the cause. This situation is understandable; it is the story of the quartermaster's life; it reflects human nature. I suspect that too often apologists for one or another general or command, or for the Confederacy itself, have overworked the logistical cliché. This surmise is not intended to evade the facts. The rebel soldier had to scrimp and scramble for everything from the first muster. He understood that it would be so. The minimum essentials were usually rounded up somehow. In the Trans-Mississippi Department, the troops, however miserable, it seems, managed better than did their brothers east of the river. No major battles were lost for want of supplies—supplies of men, yes, but not of stores. In other words, explanations for Confederate failure everywhere, certainly in the Trans-Mississippi, in my opinion, must include a complex of factors involving the whole peculiar organism "at the South." The supply services cannot be isolated for an easy indictment. The supply men in the Trans-Mississippi certainly made mistakes; a few may have been corrupt; but on the whole they appear to have been conscientious rebel patriots. Their efforts were surely among the reasons for Federal failure for four years to break up resistance in the Trans-Mississippi.

Quartermaster operations in the Trans-Mississippi are treated here under six chapter headings. Chapter I, which might have been called "Introduction," deals with definitions and examples: who and what were quartermasters and how were they related to the other branches of service? Chapters II to VI present major areas of quartermaster responsibility; they attempt to trace the development of policy with respect to each function and to report on ultimate outcomes. Chapter VII endeavors to pull the story together with a summary and set of conclusions.

Principal manuscript sources, besides the Birge Papers mentioned above, have been papers and letterbooks located at The University of Texas, the Texas State Archives, the National Archives, the New

York Historical Society, Louisiana State University, and Northwestern State College at Natchitoches, Louisiana. A few items were found in the East Texas Collection of Stephen F. Austin State College, Nacogdoches, Texas. All Civil War monographs, such as this work purports to be, are contrived around a structure of materials gleaned from the indispensable *Official Records of the Union and Confederate Armies*. The newspaper collections of The University of Texas Library, the Texas State Archives, the Arkansas History Commission, and the University of Arkansas Library provided useful contemporary reports from the press. To the efficient archivists of all these depositories, I again say thanks for their courtesies.

For suggesting the subject I am jointly indebted to Professors Lathrop and Vandiver. My greatest obligation, which I take pleasure in acknowledging, is to Professor Lathrop for his exacting demands as supervisor of my work at The University of Texas.

A grant-in-aid and relief from teaching duties, granted by colleagues at Stephen F. Austin State College for part of the summer of 1962, enabled me to get a manuscript to the publisher. My thanks go especially to President Ralph Wright Steen, Dr. C. K. Chamberlain, head of the Department of History and Government, and to Dr. Ed Kelly, chairman of the Faculty Research Committee.

My domestic colleague, my wife, Evelyn, agreeably tolerated and effectively accomplished the necessary typing.

James L. Nichols

Nacogdoches, Texas

Contents

The Confederate Quartermaster
in the
Trans-Mississippi

I

The Quartermaster: His Place and Purpose

Organizational Evolutions

An understanding of the operations of any organization, public or private, requires some knowledge of its origin and evolution. *Confederate Quartermaster's Department* and the *Trans-Mississippi* refer to two military organizations of the Confederate States of America, a supply service and a command theater, related to each other in manners prescribed by regulations and orders, general and special. Brief consideration of the development of each of these agencies should appear early therefore in any discussion of either.

The Confederate Congress, by acts dating from February, 1861, to March, 1862, established in the Confederate Army a Quartermaster's Department consisting of two general branches: quartermasters with troops in the field, and quartermasters at permanent posts and depots.[1] From 1861 to 1863 Lieutenant Colonel Abraham Charles Myers, as quartermaster general, directed the activities of his hard-pressed branch of service from Richmond. Myers, a

---

[1] J. M. Matthews (ed.), *The Statutes at Large of the Provisional Government of the Confederate States of America . . .* , p. 38; Congressional Acts of March 6, March 14, May 16, and August 29, 1861, and February 15, 1862, in W. W. Lester and W. J. Bromwell (eds.), *A Digest of the Military and Naval Laws of the Confederate States, From the Commencement of the Provisional Congress to the End of the First Congress under the Permanent Constitution*, pp. 19–20, 86–87.

controversial figure, was then replaced by Brigadier General Alexander R. Lawton, who served until the end of the war.[2] Lieutenant Colonels Larkin Smith and A. H. Cole, successive assistants in the Richmond quartermaster offices from 1863 to 1865, directed tax-in-kind collection and the manufacture and supply of field transportation equipment. From the desks of these several men came the policies which controlled in varying degrees the quartermaster officers in the Trans-Mississippi.

The evolution of military command in the Trans-Mississippi bears upon quartermaster operations there because the higher commanders played a large part in directing such operations, and because changes in the structure of command produced changes in quartermaster organization. During the first two years of the war there was no centralized command in the states west of the Mississippi. Colonel Earl Van Dorn, the ranking Confederate officer in Texas in March, 1861, set up headquarters at Indianola to raise troops. In the autumn of 1861 Brigadier General Paul O. Hébert replaced Van Dorn, assuming command of the "Military department of Texas," while Van Dorn took command of the forces gathering in Arkansas. Hébert continued in Texas, with headquarters at Houston, until the latter part of 1862. In May of 1862 all of the region west of the Mississippi became the Trans-Mississippi Department, divided into two districts. The Texas District consisted of Texas, the area to the west of Texas, and part of western Louisiana; and the Arkansas District contained Arkansas, northern Louisiana, Missouri, and the Indian Territory.[3] Major General T. C. Hindman commanded in Arkansas, and Hébert had the Texas District.

The first step toward centralization came in July, 1862, when Major General T. H. Holmes began direction of the entire Department from headquarters at Little Rock, Arkansas. District bounda-

---

[2] See Charles W. Ramsdell, "Abraham Charles Myers" in *Dictionary of American Biography*, XIII, 375; and Robert Preston Brooks, "Alexander R. Lawton," in *ibid.*, XI, 61.

[3] General Orders No. 39, Adjutant and Inspector General's Office, Richmond, in *The War of the Rebellion: A Compilation of the Official Records of the Union and Confederate Armies*, Ser. I, Vol. IX, p. 713; *ibid.*, Vol. LIII, p. 819. Hereafter cited as *Official Records*.

ries changed, and the two districts became three: Louisiana; Arkansas and the Indian Territory; and Texas (including nominally New Mexico and Arizona).[4] Major General Richard Taylor came in to command the Louisiana District while Hindman retained his command in Arkansas. Major General John B. Magruder, fresh from Lee's army in Virginia, replaced Hébert in Texas.[5] The command structure remained thus until the arrival of Lieutenant General Edmund Kirby-Smith in March, 1863. Smith moved departmental headquarters to Shreveport, Louisiana, and from that location developed such "extraordinary" powers and so many bureaus that the Trans-Mississippi became known as "Kirby-Smithdom."[6]

Quartermaster effectiveness increased as unity and system began to appear in an area initially confused. Until unification of the Trans-Mississippi under General Holmes, district quartermasters had operated independently of each other. Holmes' quartermaster, Major John D. Adams, started steps toward harmony. Later, under General Kirby-Smith's centralized command, the Quartermaster's Department in the Trans-Mississippi became specialized and divided into the Clothing Bureau, Cotton Bureau, and such variously entitled *de facto* bureaus as the Tax-in-Kind Office, Field Transportation Service, and Pay Bureau. Although the highest quartermaster authority in the Trans-Mississippi remained always Kirby-Smith's staff quartermaster at Shreveport, the main nerve center for the paper work was a Quartermaster Bureau at Marshall, directed by Lieutenant Colonel L. W. O'Bannon.[7]

[4] General Orders No. 1, Headquarters, Trans-Mississippi Department, Vicksburg, July 30, 1862, *Official Records*, Vol. XIII, p. 860; General Orders No. 5, August 20, 1862, *ibid.*, Vol. IX, p. 731.

[5] *Ibid.* Hébert remained in command of the Texas District until Magruder took command in November, 1862. See General Orders No. 1, Headquarters, District of Texas, New Mexico and Arizona, Houston, November 29, 1862, *Official Records*, Vol. XV, pp. 880–881.

[6] Joseph Howard Parks, *General Edmund Kirby Smith, C.S.A.* pp. 255 ff. See also Florence E. Holladay, "The Powers of the Commander of the Confederate Trans-Mississippi Department," *Southwestern Historical Quarterly*, XXI (January and April, 1918), 279–298, 333–359.

[7] General Orders No. 33, May 30, 1864, Confederate States Army, Trans-Mississippi Department, *General Orders, Headquarters, Trans-Mississippi Department, from March 6, 1863 to January 1, 1865*, p. 25; General Orders No. 49, *ibid.*, p. 48. Hereafter cited as *General Orders, Trans-Mississippi Department*.

Quartermaster Mission

A spokesman for the Federal quartermaster in January, 1861, declared that department "the most important by far of all the staff." [8] Major Benjamin Bloomfield, Magruder's staff quartermaster in Texas and author of a pocket guide for his service, declared the duty of a quartermaster of field troops was "to ascertain and supply their respective wants, and to treat every soldier with whom he may have business, as some absent one's darling, whose comfort and health are, to a great extent, dependent on his exertions." The quartermaster's duty to the government was "a just and correct account of all Property and money received by him, and paid out, and issued in accordance with the Regulations." [9] In the same vein, the Federal spokesman declared with a flourish:

The Quartermaster's Department . . . houses and nurses the army; makes its fire and furnishes its bed; shoes and clothes it; follows it up, with its outstretched and sheltering arms, dropping only mercies, wherever it goes; carries, even to its most distant and difficult camps, the food it eats, the clothing it wears, the cartridge it fires, the medicine it consumes; and finally, when "life's fitful fever" is over, constructs its coffin, digs its grave, conducts its burial, may even erect a head-board to mark the spot where "sleeps well" the departed hero, and keeps besides, by special Act of Congress, a record of the time and place of his interment, for future references of his friends or others. [10]

The *Army Regulations* ordered the quartermaster to provide "quarters and transportation for all army supplies; army clothing; camp and garrison equipage; cavalry and artillery horses; fuel; forage; straw, and stationery." All incidental expenses of the army were to be paid through the quartermaster—including per diem pay to extra-duty men; postage on public service; courts-martial ex-

---

[8] J. F. Rusling, "A Word for the Quartermaster's Department," *United States Service Magazine*, III (January, 1865), 57.

[9] B. Bloomfield, *The Quartermaster's Guide, Being a Compilation from the Army Regulations and Other Sources: Also the Pay Bureau of the Quartermaster's Department*, p. 3. Hereafter cited as Bloomfield, *Quartermaster's Guide*.

[10] Rusling, "A Word for the Quartermaster's Department," *United States Service Magazine*, III (January, 1865), 59.

penses; apprehension of deserters; burials of officers and men; hire of escorts, spies, interpreters and guides; veterinary services, medicines and water supply; and all other "proper and authorized expenses for the movements and operations of the Army not expressly assigned to any other department." [11] Some of these other expenses not listed were as follows: telegraphic dispatches in public service; all persons and articles hired; hospital and office furniture; harness; building materials; tools for blacksmiths, veterinarians, masons, bricklayers, and fatigue details; expendable stores such as iron, steel, ropes, and horseshoes; commutations of officers' quarters; last, and perhaps foremost, expenses of army transportation.[12]

Complete quartermaster instructions in these *Regulations* provided for authorized ration allowances of fuel, forage, transportation, stationery, and clothing, and for an accounting procedure. For example, all officers handling money or public property were required to report monthly and quarterly to the quartermaster general on nine different forms, listed as follows: a summary statement (Form 1); a report of persons and things (Form 2); a roll of extra-duty men (Form 3); a report of stores for transportation (Form 4); a return of animals, wagons, harness, etc. (Form 5); a report of forage (Form 6); a report of fuel and quarters commuted (Form 7); a report of pay due (Form 8); and an estimate of funds for one month (Form 9). These reports were routed through "channels," of course; a brigade quartermaster, for example, would forward his reports through the divisional and other appropriate quartermasters.

As each three-month period ended, each officer handling funds or quartermaster property was expected to submit a return on his account current of money (Form 10) with abstracts and vouchers (Forms 11–22); a return of property (Form 23) with abstracts and vouchers (Forms 24–45); and finally, a statement of allowances paid to officers during the quarter (Form 46). Additional completed forms, numbered 47, 48, and 22 (again), were to be included

[11] *Army Regulations Adopted for the Use of the Army of the Confederate States*, Art. XLI, pp. 120–221. For a summary of Federal quartermaster regulations and operations, see Russell F. Weigley, *Quartermaster General of the Union Army: A Biography of M. C. Meigs*, pp. 215–236.

[12] Bloomfield, *Quartermaster's Guide*, p. 22.

for money received or disbursed under "contingencies of the army." For expenses for the Medical Department, the quartermaster reported on forms 49 and 50. Each quarterly group of reports had also to include returns of clothing, camp and garrison equipage received, on hand, and issued (Form 51), and the receipt roll of issues to soldiers (Form 52).[13] All these forms and reports undoubtedly added up to a careful system of records and accounting. The mere listing of them is almost overwhelming.

If the quartermaster officer was detailed to act as paymaster, he had also to handle forms of the Pay Bureau in accordance with its regulations. After each payment he was to submit an estimate of funds for succeeding months (Form 54); an abstract of payments (Form 60) with vouchers; a general account current in duplicate (Form 61); and a monthly statement of funds, disbursements, etc., on Form 63. To complicate his work even further, separate accounts and reports were made for regular army expenses and for those of volunteer and militia troops.[14]

Truly, the Department was assigned a massive mission, including many functions nowadays assigned to other branches of the services of supply, but in 1861 the only other major supply services were the Ordnance Bureau and the Commissary Department. Guns, gunpowder, and groceries would concern these last two, while the quartermaster had to search for almost everything else in a region almost completely agrarian. Existing transportation and industrial facilities amounted to little in the Trans-Mississippi. Less than 1,000 miles of railroad could be found in the entire area, compared to 1,400 in Georgia or 1,800 in Virginia.[15] Especially wanting was a track to the Rio Grande, from whence would have to come supplies from Europe via Matamoros.

Captain N. A. Birge, Typical Post Quartermaster

Any quartermaster officer stationed at a supply or transportation depot in the early years of the war was usually termed *post quarter-*

---

[13] *Regulations of the Army of the Confederate States, 1862: Containing a Complete Set of Forms*, pp. 80–81. Hereafter cited as *Regulations*. Illustrations of all forms used were printed in the *Regulations*, pp. 83–138.

[14] *Ibid.*, pp. 81–82.

[15] Robert C. Black, III, *Railroads of the Confederacy*, pp. 3–4.

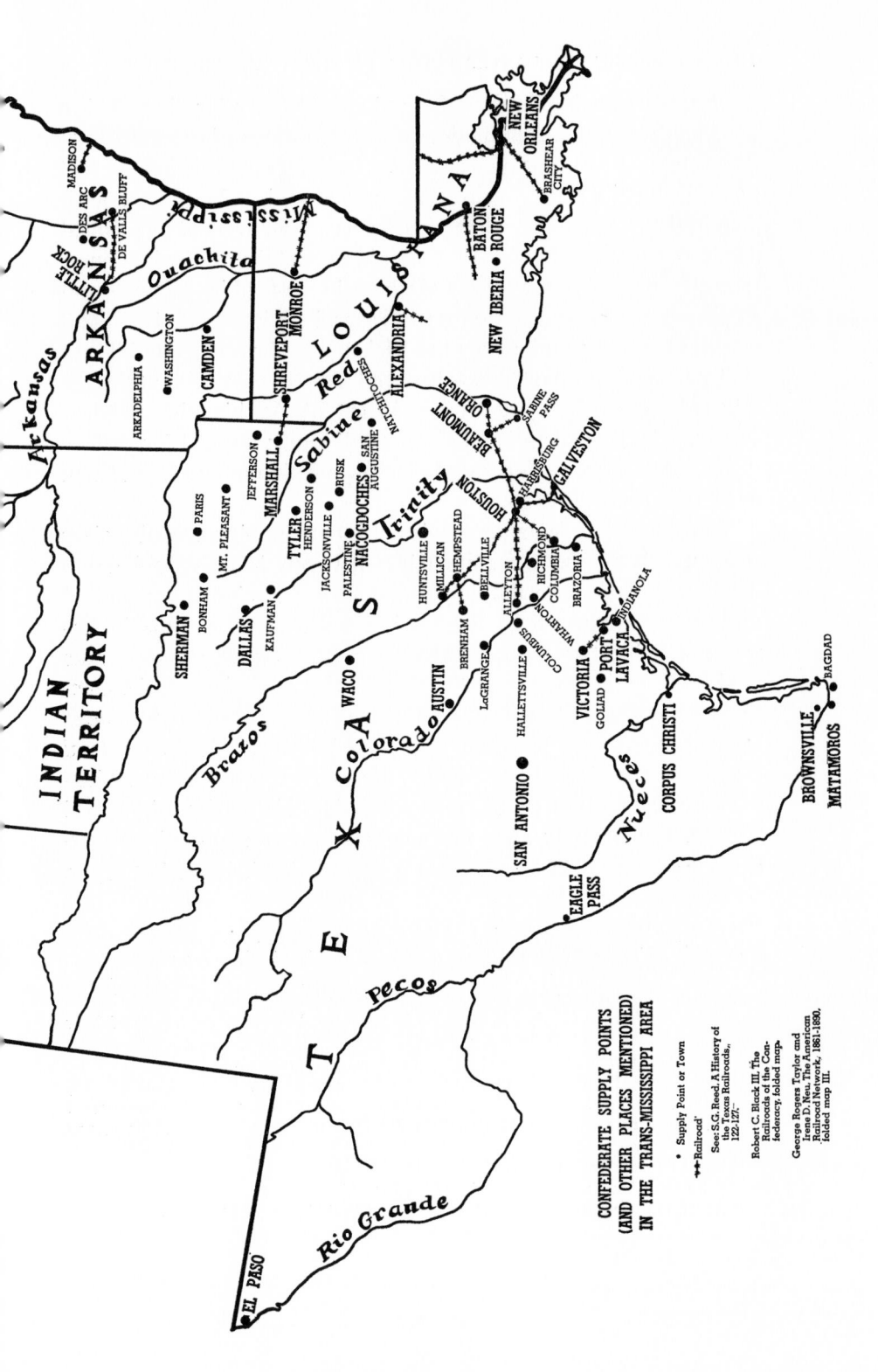

MADISON
DES ARC
LITTLE ROCK
DE VALLS BLUFF

ARKANSAS

Ouachita

Arkansas

WASHINGTON
CAMDEN
ARKADELPHIA

INDIAN TERRITORY

SHERMAN
BONHAM
PARIS
MT. PLEASANT
JEFFERSON
MARSHALL
DALLAS
KAUFMAN
TYLER
HENDERSON
JACKSONVILLE
RUSK
PALESTINE
NACOGDOCHES
SAN AUGUSTINE
NATCHITOCHES

SHREVEPORT
MONROE

LOUISIANA

Red

Sabine

ALEXANDRIA

Mississippi

NEW ORLEANS
BRASHEAR CITY
BATON ROUGE
NEW IBERIA

Trinity

ORANGE
BEAUMONT
SABINE PASS
HOUSTON
HARRISBURG
GALVESTON

HUNTSVILLE
MILLICAN
HEMPSTEAD
BELLVILLE
ALLEYTON
RICHMOND
COLUMBIA
BRAZORIA
WHARTON
COLUMBUS
PORT LAVACA
INDIANOLA
VICTORIA
GOLIAD

BRENHAM
LaGRANGE
HALLETTSVILLE

T E X A S

Brazos

Colorado

WACO
AUSTIN

SAN ANTONIO

Nueces

CORPUS CHRISTI

BAGDAD
BROWNSVILLE
MATAMOROS

EAGLE PASS

Pecos

Rio Grande

EL PASO

**CONFEDERATE SUPPLY POINTS
(AND OTHER PLACES MENTIONED)
IN THE TRANS-MISSISSIPPI AREA**

• Supply Point or Town
✚✚ Railroad

See: S.G. Reed, A History of
the Texas Railroads,
122-127.

Robert C. Black III, The
Railroads of the Con-
federacy, folded map.

George Rogers Taylor and
Irene D. Neu, The American
Railroad Network, 1861-1890,
folded map III.

master. Since such officers performed almost every function cited in the *Regulations,* an examination of the operations of Captain N. A. Birge, typical assistant quartermaster in the Trans-Mississippi, will serve to illustrate the system. Birge was placed at Monroe, Louisiana, in the fall of 1862, when Quartermaster General Myers named Monroe, Little Rock, and Arkadelphia as the "three principal quartermaster posts" for the supply of troops in the field in Arkansas and Louisiana.[16] The post at Monroe was especially important because it was the western terminus for the Vicksburg, Shreveport and Texas Railroad. Despite the "Shreveport and Texas" part of the title, the railroad extended only to Monroe in 1862.[17] At this railhead Birge supervised a large depot and shops of all kinds; he paid for various items and services and operated as transportation officer for the area until mid-June in 1863.[18]

Transportation demands required Birge to employ available river steamers plying the Ouachita River between Monroe and Arkadelphia, Arkansas, to the north, and Bayou Teche to the south.[19] Orders were to use light-draught boats whenever possible in forwarding freight from Monroe to the north.[20] Among the steamers used by Captain Birge were the *Cornie,* the *Twilight,* and the *General Beauregard.*[21] A typical use of these steamers occurred between December 25 and 31 when Captain Lin Moore of the *General Beauregard* carried a large quantity of government stores from Monroe to a safer place up the Ouachita. For this service Birge paid $3,000. Immediately after this emergency movement, Birge chartered the boat again to transport a part of the Arizona Battery to

[16] General Papers of the Period of the Confederacy, Case 12, Archives of The University of Texas Library. Unless otherwise noted, all Birge references are to this collection, hereafter cited as Birge Papers. Some portions of the present account of Captain Birge at Monroe were previously published by this writer in *Louisiana Studies,* I (Fall, 1962), 23–29. See also Myers to Secretary of War Randolph, July 9, 1862, *Official Records,* Ser. I, Vol. XIII, p. 854.

[17] Birge's Report for the First Quarter, 1863, Birge Papers, Case 14.

[18] *Ibid.,* Case 15. Birge's ledger record of transportation tickets paid by rail, stage, and boat is a significant item found in a group of papers styled "Confederate States Army Collection (I) 1860–65" in the Department of Archives, Louisiana State University.

[19] Birge Papers, Case 12.

[20] John D. Adams to Birge, October 16, 1862, *ibid.,* Case 12.

[21] Receipts for payment for services are found in *ibid.,* Cases 12, 13, 14.

Rosedale—a movement directed by General Taylor.[22] The *Cornie,*
appearing on Birge's reports as public property, was used by the
quartermaster as a salt boat plying between Monroe and the salt
works in southern Louisiana.[23] These works were probably the extremely valuable Avery Island mines near New Iberia.[24] They produced twenty-two million pounds of rock salt for the Confederacy
during the year before their capture by the Federals in 1863.[25]

In addition to his water transport, Birge kept wagon trains going
continuously between Monroe and the northern area, moving every
type of item to the combat troops in Arkansas. For this purpose 303
mules, 54 wagons, and 9 ambulances were based at Monroe while
all wagons arriving from the field or from the Arkadelphia post were
loaded with suitable items for return trips. Shipments during October to the Camden, Arkansas, quartermaster included 28 cases of
guns, 25 cases of clothing, 2 cases of officer's swords, 1 case of
bayonets and scabbards, 4 cases of medicines, and 40 cases of tea. A
similar shipment started north near the end of the month.[26] A contin-
uous stream of these shipments flowed from Monroe during the fall
and winter of 1862.[27]

Birge's transportation function included the payment of all types
of service bills and expenses relative to railroads, and buggy or
wagon rentals. The Vicksburg, Shreveport and Texas Railroad
Company carried a large quantity of freight to and from Monroe.
During January, 1863, for example, approximately 1,100 soldiers
rode these rails, along with freight, at a cost of $5,562.55.[28] A hired
buggy, used to carry Brigadier General A. G. Blanchard to the

[22] John D. Adams to Birge, October 16, 1862, in *ibid.,* Case 13; Special Orders
No. 1, Headquarters Military District North Louisiana, January 1, 1863, *ibid.,*
Case 14.
[23] "Monthly Return of Public Animals, Wagons, Harness and Other Means of
Transportation," October, 1862, *ibid.,* Case 12.
[24] Ella Lonn, *Salt as a Factor in the Confederacy,* p. 32.
[25] E. Merton Coulter, *The Confederate States of America, 1861–1865,* pp.
247–248. Birge may have been hauling salt from works in Winn Parish. See also
John Q. Anderson (ed.), *Brokenburn, The Journal of Kate Stone, 1861–1868,* p.
170.
[26] Return for October, 1862, Birge Papers, Case 12.
[27] List of shipments for October, 1862, *ibid.*
[28] Abstract B., First Quarter, 1863, "The Confederate States to the V. S. & Texas
Railroad Co.," January, 1863 (paid February 4), Birge Papers, Case 14.

mouth of the Red River to supervise the erection of fortifications, cost the government $51.00. On another occasion, Birge hastily hired wagons and teams to haul sabers to the 30th Texas Cavalry Regiment at Waco, Texas. Procured, somehow, by government agents, the sabers had been delivered to Birge at Monroe.[29]

The success of Birge at Monroe and of his associates at Arkadelphia and Little Rock was recognized by Quartermaster General Myers in July, 1862, when he reported that these posts and facilities provided adequate transportation for troops in the area. Government equipage in the Trans-Mississippi, Myers stated, could accommodate 30,000 men.[30]

Although *Regulations* authorized all quartermasters to purchase appropriate items, the Richmond office, in a circular directive in March, 1863, provided for coordination of effort in the Trans-Mississippi. A principal purchasing officer was named for each state: one for Texas at San Antonio, one for Arkansas at Little Rock, and one for Louisiana at Alexandria. Captain Birge's relation to these officers was fixed as follows:

Quartermasters stationed at the various posts within either of said purchasing districts will be the subordinate purchasing officers therein, and before buying supplies or contracting therefor they will confer with the principal officer and conform to such general or specific instructions as he may give respecting the price, quantity or quality of the supplies to be bought.[31]

Quartermasters of the armies in the field received orders to avoid competing with purchasing officers and to cooperate with and draw from them. An exception would be forage and fuel, which could best be found in the field of operation. The field-army quartermasters could purchase other items if absolutely necessary, but in no instance were they or the state or post purchasing officers to compete with ordnance procurement of hides, leather, harnesses, etc.[32]

[29] Colonel E. J. Gurley to Birge, October 8, 1862, *ibid.,* Case 12.
[30] Myers to Secretary of War Randolph, July 9, 1862, *Official Records,* Ser. I, Vol. XIII, p. 854.
[31] Circular, Quartermaster General's Office, March 24, 1863, *ibid.,* Vol. XXX, Pt. IV, pp. 683–686.
[32] *Ibid.,* p. 684.

Quartermaster reports, especially the grand consolidated monthly, were exceptionally irksome to Captain Birge because his activities were so varied. Consequently, in December, 1862, he wrote Trans-Mississippi Chief Quartermaster John D. Adams for relief:

> The affairs of this Post are often very much scattered; as for instance, I have now agents off at the Salt works, hiring wagon & teams, to send salt to Texas and other points, which renders it impossible to make a direct statement of Persons and Articles employed. If however, other Quartermasters, similarly situated, are required such returns, I will endeavor to make the same, as correct as possible under the circumstances.[33]

Instead of giving relief, Major W. L. Cabell, successor to Adams in 1863, added a number of local reports for the use of his office.[34] These local reports, apparently in addition to the long list regularly required by *Regulations,* were as follows: (1) monthly summary statement, (2) report of persons and articles hired, (3) report of public animals and wagons.[35]

Items manufactured at Monroe included almost every type of quartermaster article. Birge's report for the three-month period of April to June listed the following: [36]

Quantity	Item	Quantity	Item
101	shoe lasts	2	vests
520 lbs.	leather	49	jackets
148	sacks	462 prs.	shoes
2	tent flys	5	boots
58 prs.	pants	31	coffins
864	drawers	86	haversacks
883	shirts	39	wool hats

Wagon beds, boring tools, benches, lathes, harness, chains, and miscellaneous items.

---

[33] Birge to Major John D. Adams, December 10, 1862, Birge Papers, Case 13.

[34] Circular of December 31, 1862, *Arkansas Patriot* (Little Rock), January 8, 1863. Major, later Brigadier General, Cabell had been chief quartermaster at the First Battle of Manassas. In that role, immediately after the battle, Cabell, on orders from Generals Beauregard and Johnston, arranged for the manufacture of the well-known Confederate battle flags. Official flags "Stars and Bars" used on the Manassas field had been too difficult to identify and to distinguish from the Federal "Stars and Stripes." W. L. Cabell to [J. S. Sargent?], January 12, 1910

The item *coffins* on the above list reflects the obligation of the quartermaster for all burial expenses. Burial of soldiers dying in the post hospital at Monroe was provided by Birge's shops, the coffins being issued on requisition from the hospital.[37]

In June, 1863, Captain Birge was ordered to Shreveport to establish "the necessary Shops for the Manufacture of Wagons [,] Ambulances, also Clothing and Camp and Garrison Equipage." Major W. H. Haynes of the Clothing Bureau, whose operations are treated in some detail in a subsequent chapter, was to be Birge's supervisor in such parts of this order as pertained to his Bureau.[38] As in Monroe, however, the manufacture and storage of clothing was to be only a part of the post quartermaster's operations. Although transportation and the payment of various expenses were still important concerns, most of Birge's time was probably occupied with general supervision of his extensive shops and large number of personnel. Approximately 160 men were assigned or hired under Birge to serve in the shops and office or with the teams. Of this number, approximately 100 men were enlisted personnel detailed to the post by Generals Kirby-Smith, Blanchard, or T. H. Holmes. Fifty men were employed as follows: 1 as shoemaker, 8 as wagonmakers, 3 as blacksmiths, 6 as harness makers, 7 as tailors, 1 as wagon master, 17 as teamsters, 1 as stableman, 3 as clerks, 2 as assistant storekeepers, and 1 as shop superintendent. The second group of approximately 60 men included whites and Negroes. The Negroes were hired from their owners, or, as in the case of 6 of them, were captured from the Federals. The stable superintendent, yardmaster, and forage master were white, but the others, including carpenters, blacksmiths, teamsters, hostlers, strikers, and laborers, were black.[39]

(letter privately owned, microfilm copy in possession of this writer); W. L. Cabell, "True History of Our Battle Flag," *Confederate Veteran,* XI (August, 1903), 1; Mr. Earle Cabell to this writer, December 26, 1961; Lucille Dufner, "The Flags of the Confederate States of America" (unpublished M.A. thesis).

[35] Circular of December 31, 1862, *Arkansas Patriot,* January 8, 1863.

[36] Birge Papers, Case 15.

[37] *Ibid.,* Case 12.

[38] Special Orders No. 51, Headquarters Trans-Mississippi Department, June 10, 1863, *ibid.*

[39] "Report of Persons and Articles Employed and Hired at Shreveport, Louisiana, July, 1863," Birge Papers, Case 15.

Eleven quartermaster buildings, housing the varied occupations, were employed as follows: [40]

> 1 for tailor shop and store
> 1 " blacksmith shop
> 1 " storeroom
> 1 " quartermaster office
> 1 " shoe shop
> 1 " wood and blacksmith shop
> 1 " storeroom and saddle shop
> 1 " stablehands' quarters
> 1 " forage house
> 1 (including lot) for horses
> 1 "   "   for stable

With the above-listed personnel and facilities, Birge manufactured a large list of equipment in July and August of 1863. Among the articles completed were 15 wagon beds, 91 soapboxes and breadboxes, packing boxes, coffins, shoes, wagonsheets, pincers, tongs, shoes and shoe lasts, benches, peg cutters, pillowslips, jackets, etc. All types of clothing were fabricated for the Clothing Bureau.[41] The output was typical of any two months' work at the post, and when multiplied by the number of similar posts in the Department, the contribution was undoubtedly significant.

The foregoing description of the duties and functions of one post quartermaster during the years 1862 and 1863 indicates that nearly all of the responsibilities listed for the quartermaster were performed at the permanent posts and depots. That this was a tremendous burden on one system of officers can be seen when the scope of their work is comprehended; and, consequently, as later chapters of this study will indicate, the Quartermaster's Department was forced to organize "bureaucratically" so that major concerns might be handled by specialists.

[40] *Ibid.*
[41] *Ibid.*

II

Clothing and Equipage

Ideals and Realities

Confederate clothing plans in March, 1861, required the eager volunteer to come to the colors clothed and equipped at his own expense. Congress promised to repay him for his outfit at the rate of $21.00 for each six-month period of service.[1] If the volunteer companies had received part of their clothing from the Confederate States, they were reimbursed only a commuted sum for the items furnished by individual members or benefactors. The commutation system was eventually abolished completely, however, as the individual soldier found it impossible to obtain adequate clothes for himself.[2] He would never cease trying, certainly, and he would wear what he could get, whatever the source.

The quartermaster, meanwhile, under a congressional order of August, 1861, sought to eliminate deficiencies where they existed. The Secretary of War paid individual states for equipment furnished by them for their own troops. With the abolition of the commutation system in 1862, the Quartermaster's Department received, unquali-

---

[1] This figure was later increased to $25.00. See Lester and Bromwell, *Digest of Military and Naval Laws,* pp. 91–92.

[2] Charles W. Ramsdell, "The Control of Manufacturing by the Confederate Government," *Mississippi Valley Historical Review,* VIII (December, 1921), 232.

fiedly, full responsibility for clothing allowances for all troops in Confederate service. If the Department failed to fill the quotas, soldiers received payment in cash for the deficiency.[3]

The War Department, in the *Regulations* in 1862, detailed a table of clothing allowances per soldier. The table, a seldom realized ideal, authorized uniform clothing as listed "or articles thereof of equal value": [4]

Clothing	For Three Years 1st	2nd	3rd	Total in Three Years	Price per Article
Cap, complete	2	1	1	4	$ 2.00
Cover	1	1	1	3	.38
Coat	2	1	1	4	12.00
Trousers	3	2	2	7	9.00
Flannel shirts	3	3	3	9	3.00
Flannel drawers	3	2	2	7	3.00
Bootees, pairs	4	4	4	12	6.00
Stockings	4	4	4	12	1.00
Leather stock	1			1	.25
Great coat	1			1	25.00
Stable frock (for mounted men)	1			1	2.00
Fatigue overall (for engineers and ordnance men)	1	1	1	3	3.00
Blanket	1		1	2	7.50

Other items to be provided were sashes (for each sergeant), metallic letters, numbers, castles, shells, and other insignia of service branches. *Regulations* directed company commanders to draw clothing for their men twice a year ordinarily, or more often if circumstances required. Regimental commanders approved clothing requisitions which were consolidated by their quartermasters and

[3] Lester and Bromwell, *Digest of Military and Naval Laws,* p. 92.

[4] *Regulations of the Army of the Confederate States, 1862,* p. 79. The prices given are as established in General Orders No. 100, Adjutant and Inspector General's Office, Richmond, December 8, 1862, *Official Records,* Ser. IV, Vol. II, p. 230.

forwarded to divisional quartermasters for procurement. A muster roll of issues at company level carried the account of each man.[5]

Generally speaking, ready-made clothing could not be found in the South in 1861. When the quartermaster received cloth in bulk, he either turned it over to women volunteers to be sewed, or he hired help to convert the material into clothing. This putting-out system proved to be unsatisfactory, and by the end of the first year almost all government clothing was made under supervision in quartermaster shops.[6]

To aid in the change in policy, Congress authorized the executive to import, duty free, cards and card-cloth or any machinery or materials necessary to increase the manufacture of clothing.[7] Any color or quality of cloth became a uniform for Confederate troops. They had begun in a glamorous variety of regalia in 1861, and the hodgepodge continued, although increasingly less glamorous. Freedom from regulation ideals became more pronounced as the years passed, and in 1863 the predominant uniform color came to be not cadet-gray, but "butternut." Such a distinctive color resulted from the use of a dye made of copperas and walnut hulls.[8]

Trans-Mississippi Troops and Clothes, 1861–1862

In the first months of 1861 no organized Confederate command existed in the Trans-Mississippi to systematize the mustering process and the results were perforce piecemeal, with each state trying to clothe and equip the men it called into service to meet Confederate quotas. In Texas, Governor Edward Clark hastily raised twenty companies for Virginia service, promising that the men would be equipped in Virginia if they could not complete their wardrobes before they left.[9]

The first recruiting rush over, Texas set up a system in September,

---

[5] *Regulations of the Army . . . 1862,* pp. 79–80.

[6] Ramsdell, "The Control of Manufacturing by the Confederate Government," *Mississippi Valley Historical Review,* VIII (December, 1921), 232.

[7] Lester and Bromwell, *Digest of Military and Naval Laws,* pp. 92–93.

[8] Bell I. Wiley, *The Life of Johnny Reb,* p. 111.

[9] Adjutant General S. Cooper to Brigadier General Van Dorn, June 12, 1861, *Official Records,* Ser. I, Vol. IV, p. 91; *Dallas Herald,* July 17, 1861.

1861, to organize popular aid. Governor Clark asked each county to form a clothing society. Confederate bonds were promised as ultimate recompense for all "donations." Depots under special agents were established at Jefferson, Henderson, Palestine, Dallas, Sherman, Waco, Austin, San Antonio, Victoria, Houston, and Beaumont to receive the contributions.[10] Newspapers in all sections seconded the state's appeal, saying that particular urgency existed to supply men already in the field, who faced a cold winter in Arkansas and elsewhere.[11]

Several effective "ladies' societies" already had partially equipped a number of units. One society in Houston, for example, from May 15 to October, 1861, made for Texas volunteers:

85 suits, coats and pants for the Bayou City Guards
84 "   "   "   "   "   " Confederate Guards
6 "   "   "   "   "   " Gentry Volunteers
12 "   "   "   "   "   " Davis Guards
5 "   "   "   "   "   " Houston Artillery
20 "   "   "   "   "   " Hickory Cavalry
20 flannel shirts for the Archer Grays
40 tents (20 double-type)
520 flannel shirts and drawers
83 pairs cotton drawers
40 pairs wool socks, knit
30 comforts

In addition to these items, the society purchased 72 flannel shirts, 120 pairs of drawers, and 72 pairs of socks. Donations of manufactured or used items were not put on the list, but undoubtedly many of these also went into the Governor's depots.[12]

---

[10] *Bellville Countryman,* September 25, 1861; *Official Records,* Ser. I, Vol. IV, pp. 102–103. Agents appointed were W. P. Saufley, Jefferson; J. H. Parsons, Henderson; A. E. McClure, Palestine; Dr. Samuel Pryor, Dallas; W. E. Sanders, Sherman; J. W. Speight, Waco; W. H. D. Carrington, Austin; Vance and Bros., San Antonio; William S. Glass, Victoria; E. W. Taylor, Houston; John H. Herring, Beaumont.

[11] *Dallas Herald,* November 25, 1861; *Bellville Countryman,* October 2, 1861.

[12] *Houston Tri-Weekly Telegraph,* October 20, 1861, cited by Robert P. Felgar, "Texas in the War for Southern Independence" (unpublished Ph.D. dissertation), p. 419.

In some cases the ladies concentrated their effort on providing for a single unit. For example, the Ladies' Aid Society of Lancaster and vicinity, by November, 1861, had sent the regiment of Colonel B. W. Stone $1,676.50 worth of clothing and miscellany, itemized as follows: [13]

- 28 overcoats and undercoats
- 121 flannel and linsey shirts
- 112 pairs line jeans
- 120 pairs heavy winter drawers
- 27 winter vests
- 225 pairs heavy-yarn socks
- 24 pairs boots and shoes
- 28 pairs woolen mittens
- 65 bed comforters, blankets, quilts, and counterpanes

    Miscellaneous items such as neck comforters, bandages, needles, pins, towels, etc.

The ladies of Jefferson, the center of northeast Texas activity, worked for a procession of units originating in that area. A visiting Alabaman, Mrs. William Roberts, writing her niece, probably reflected the feelings of many Trans-Mississippi women as she reported on the local scene:

When will this horrid war end? That is what we can't tell and how; God only knows. It is certainly the most unjust one that ever occurred. Oh, how distressing to have our families torn up and those who are near and dear to us exposed to the cannon and gun, but all we can do is to give them up to God and plead with him to protect and shield them from all harm—this I constantly do but I feel many miserable hours I do assure you. My daughter and I have done a good deal of work for the soldiers. The ladies generally worked very well. There have been several companies started from here—the last flag presented had the motto on it—Justice or Death. Tuesday we want to go to the presenting of one. That company will go to Missouri—will leave in the evening. The first company that left here was a new thing to us and a good many of our town folks left. We went in the morning to see the banner presented and again in the evening to see them take the boat. It was the most affecting

[13] *Dallas Herald,* November 20, 1861.

scene I ever witnessed except at a funeral service—to see the parents take leave of their children. I spent the day—most of it in tears.[14]

In Marshall, to the south in Harrison County, the Ladies' Volunteer Relief Association opened operations in November with a treasury made up of members' dues of twenty-five cents each. Bandages were declared a first objective while the society secretary began to "write to the Captain of each company" asking him to list articles needed by his men. The group met every Tuesday morning at 10 o'clock at the courthouse.[15] Famous recipients of much of the product of all this effort were the W. P. Lane Rangers, whose historian recorded the gratitude of the unit when two wagonloads of clothing arrived for the men at San Antonio. Such "dear kind friends" would "never be forgotten," he wrote.[16]

Unit quartermasters with troops had Confederate funds by the end of 1861 with which to buy equipage from local hardware and general store sources. At Jefferson, Texas, for example, Captain N. A. Birge, quartermaster for the 1st Texas Battalion of Cavalry (Crump's), purchased repeatedly during that winter and spring from the firm of W. H. Nichols (a partnership of brothers).[17] Items included all kinds of engineer's tools such as wrenches, draw knives, adzes, axes, squares, augers, braces, rope, chains, iron rods and bars, and also kitchen equipment.[18]

Pleased with Texas' success in arranging for initial supply, Secretary of War Benjamin urged Governor Clark to continue his plan and to receive the Confederate cash commutation for each man supplied.[19]

[14] Mrs. William Roberts to "niece," Jefferson, Texas, November 24, 1861. Original letter in the possession of Mrs. James W. Stevenson, Victoria, Texas; typed copy in possession of the writer.

[15] *Texas Republican* (Marshall, Texas), November 26, 1861, reproduced in *News Messenger* (Marshall), November 26, 1961.

[16] William W. Heartsill, *Fourteen Hundred and 91 Days, in the Confederate Army: A Journal Kept by (above) for Four Years, One Month, and One Day, Or Camp Life, Day-By-Day, of the W. P. Lane Rangers, From April 19, 1861, to May 20, 1865,* pp. 44–45.

[17] Ancestors of the writer.

[18] From several receipts and quarterly returns, bearing dates from November 4, 1861, to March 6, 1862, Birge Papers, Case 11.

[19] Benjamin to Clark, October 13, 1861, *Official Records,* Ser. I, Vol. IV, p. 120.

In Arkansas, as in Texas, private and public agencies tried to equip volunteers before transferring them to Confederate command. A mass meeting in Van Buren brought forth a plan for local assumption of responsibility for the clothing of companies. Notable first results included the efforts of one man, Mr. James E. Woolsay, of Crawford County, who personally supplied one entire company with shoes.[20] W. L. Gammage, surgeon and historian of the 4th Arkansas Regiment, reported his outfit well supplied in August, 1861, with "good home-made tents" and transportation, although the latter appeared to be inadequate, he said, for the volume of baggage brought from home by the men.[21] The Arkansas Military Board (a creature of the Secession Convention), consisting of the governor and two advisors, contracted, under the War Department's commutation arrangement, to equip Arkansas troops before their formal muster.[22]

State military forces in Louisiana, with equipment and arms, joined Confederate service on March 15, 1861.[23] Parish public appropriations went far toward having some of the various "Grays" handsomely attired on first muster.[24] In Louisiana, too, ladies' groups knitted and sewed away. Notable examples included the New Orleans Society of Ladies in Aid, which met daily in its workshop at the Y.M.C.A. building, and the Ladies Volunteer Aid Association of Lafourche, which worked mainly for the Lafourche Creoles.[25] Kate Stone, that literate young lady of Brokenburn Plantation, near Milliken's Bend, Louisiana, in her charming wartime diary describes the concentration on knitting in her family circle in September, 1861:

[20] David Y. Thomas, *Arkansas in War and Reconstruction, 1861–1874*, p. 92. The *Semi-Weekly Citizen* (Des Arc, Arkansas), July 20, 1861, reminding volunteers that the Confederate government did not furnish clothes, urged men to go to the colors already equipped for at least ninety days' service.

[21] W. L. Gammage, *The Camp, the Bivouac, and the Battlefield*, p. 15.

[22] *Journal of Both Sessions of the Convention of the State of Arkansas*, pp. 190–250; Hardee to Adjutant General S. Cooper, July 17, 1861, *Official Records*, Ser. I, Vol. III, p. 609; Secretary of War Walker to Governor Rector, August 8, 1861, *ibid.*, p. 635; Hardee to Rector, July 25, 1861, *ibid.*, pp. 614–615.

[23] Act approved by Governor Thomas O. Moore on that date, *ibid.*, Ser. IV, Vol. I, pp. 172–173.

[24] Jefferson Davis Bragg, *Louisiana in the Confederacy*, p. 56.

[25] *Ibid.*, pp. 56–57, 87, 92.

All the boys are at work knitting with bones except Brother Coley and he is ambitious to learn. Other Pa learned when he was a little boy and has taught them, and he has knitted a complete glove today with long fingers. The gloves are for the soldiers and we are leaving the ends of the fingers open so that they can handle their guns well.[26]

Although some complaints of want continued to appear into the autumn, Trans-Mississippi quartermaster depots had enough inventory by the end of the year to satisfy congressional investigators. A. T. Bledsoe, War Department bureau chief, reported supplies would be adequate for the remainder of the winter if citizen and state contributions continued to supplement quartermaster effort at previous rates.[27] The remark of a Southern officer at the Battle of Wilson's Creek, August 10, 1861, that the Confederates were without tents, blankets, "nor any clothes, except the few we had on our backs, and four-fifths barefooted" [28] leads to the probable conclusion that supplies from home either had quickly given out in training or had been abandoned by the men as being burdensome in the heat of summer.

Commanders in Texas, Brigadier Generals H. H. Sibley and P. O. Hébert, at San Antonio and Houston, claimed to have operated with little or no quartermaster help in 1861. Sibley reported that his forces had endured the entire New Mexico campaign without receiving one dollar of quartermaster funds. His men had managed, however, to be fully equipped, he said and he added that they were again well clad at the moment of writing (May 4, 1862).[29] The success of these men keeping at least clad apparently derived from the continued efforts of the San Antonio distaff organization. In July, 1861, the San Antonio Ladies' Southern Aid Society had raised $1,282 for Sibley's brigade. These ladies, assisted by the Austin chapter, also sent 707 garments to Sibley.[30]

[26] John Q. Anderson (ed.), *Brokenburn, The Journal of Kate Stone, 1861–1868,* p. 55.
[27] A. T. Bledsoe to Moore, July 31, 1861, *Official Records,* Ser. IV, Vol. I, p. 512.
[28] Frank Cunningham, *General Stand Watie's Confederate Indians,* p. 40.
[29] Sibley to Cooper, May 4, 1862, *Official Records,* Ser. I, Vol. IX, pp. 506–507.
[30] Lois Council Ellsworth, "San Antonio During the Civil War" (unpublished M.A. thesis), p. 97. One of Sibley's men recalled a shortage of "clothing, blankets

The several post quartermasters in Texas, meanwhile, purchased and supervised local manufacture of items of equipage and clothing. Captains J. P. McKinney and William Prescott, at Austin and San Antonio, for example, advertised for socks, paying fifty cents per pair for cotton socks and sixty cents for woolen ones. McKinney's 1862 quarterly reports are exemplified in the following list of purchases, valued at $6,531.57: [31]

Item	No. Purchased
Shoes	720 pairs
Axes	59
Axe helves	60
Spades	5
Camp kettles	27
Tin pans	264
Hatchets	25
Sibley tents	44
Wall tents	3
Common tents	1
Sibley tent poles, sets	36
Wall tent poles, sets	3
Common tent poles, sets	101
Tent pins	121
Pick axes	4
Iron pots	2
Skillets and lids	15
Fry pans	38
Grub hoes	7
Coffee pots	100
Canteens	400
Water buckets	1
Ovens and lids	11

and no place to draw from . . ." Martin Hardwick Hall, *Sibley's New Mexico Campaign,* p. 38. But supplies came from somewhere, only to be lost to the Federals at Glorieta Pass. Mamie Yeary (comp.), *Reminiscences of the Boys in Gray, 1861–1865,* pp. 612–613.

[31] Quoted from *Semi-Weekly News* (San Antonio), September 1, 1862, by Ellsworth, in "San Antonio During the Civil War" (unpublished M.A. thesis), p. 38. See also portfolio marked "Miscellaneous, Department of Quartermaster and Commissary of the State of Texas and the Confederate States, 1861–1865," Archives of the State of Texas.

Captain McKinney noted his personal supervision of the manufacture of 12 pillowcases, 9 sheets, 109 corn sacks, and 2 auger handles.[32]

In the latter part of 1862 the Richmond government appointed Major Simeon Hart, a flour manufacturer of El Paso, general purchasing agent for Texas, as officials recognized the importance of obtaining supplies through Mexico. Hart was commissioned in the Quartermaster's Department and told to operate from San Antonio, purchasing for all of the services. Both the Quartermaster and the Ordnance Departments placed requisitions with him for the requirements of the Trans-Mississippi area.[33] In such a position Hart was regarded as an agency of supply by quartermasters interested in procuring clothing through imports. The government promised funds to Hart but foresaw the value of cotton as a medium for exchange.[34] Hart operated in this general purchasing capacity until the end of the war, but as his operations were so closely connected with those of the Cotton Bureau, his work will be discussed more fully in Chapter IV.

The approaching winter of 1862–1863 found Trans-Mississippi troops still woefully short of everything in spite of the combined efforts of all agencies. General Theophilus H. Holmes, departmental commander at Little Rock, summarized his straits to the War Department:

The troops are in a great measure destitute of clothing, with no prospect of supply from abroad, and dependent almost entirely upon local and domestic manufactures, which must be promptly paid for, as the people who furnish them are generally poor and cannot extend a credit.[35]

Holmes declared the complete lack of funds crippled all efforts of his quartermasters, a complaint often heard among Trans-Mississippi officers throughout the war. Hébert had complained earlier that his quartermaster accounts sold in the market for fifty cents on

[32] List No. 1, Abstract N, in portfolio marked "Quartermaster Supplies Purchased 1861–1865," Archives of the State of Texas.

[33] Secretary of War Randolph to Hart, November 14, 1862, *Official Records*, Ser. I, Vol. XV, p. 866.

[34] *Ibid.*

[35] Holmes to Randolph, September 8, 1862, *ibid.*, Vol. XIII, p. 877.

the dollar. When Governor Francis R. Lubbock of Texas pressed the War Department on the matter, Quartermaster General Myers argued that $3,158,842.32 had been sent to Texas since October 10, 1861, for the use of local quartermasters. Myers presumed this [36] to be a sufficient sum—and, had it got through to the right people, it probably would have been. A mysterious business this, trying to reconcile Richmond's confidence with the array of complaints against purchasing officers; the funds always seemed to be late. Surely, with quartermaster accounts kept with the precision indicated, the "leaky bucket" charge must be discounted. One result of the discussion between Lubbock and Myers was the removal by Myers of Captain John D. Adams as chief quartermaster of the Trans-Mississippi.[37] In any case, the time lag in distribution of funds probably contributed to lack of confidence in quartermaster credit.

Combat troop quartermasters or their agents from Arkansas or Tennessee occasionally appeared in home locales to load up with whatever donations families and friends could manage for the return trip. A newspaper notice, dated November, 1862, offers an example of this direct type of procurement:

Clothing for Arkansas

W. H. Maples, Agent for Clothing for Colonel Hawp's [Hawpe's] regiment of Texas Cavalry, now in Arkansas, will receive the same at Sampson & Hendricks' Store, Austin, Texas, until Monday evening, next, November 3. Those having clothing, blankets, &c., to send, will please deliver them at once, as the wagon will positively leave on Tuesday morning.[38]

The unit wagons carrying donations, such as these, either public or private, operating outside post or Clothing Bureau control, continued to be major vehicles of troop supply throughout the war. A contemporary observer later regarded "this patriotic method" the

---

[36] Lubbock to Benjamin, March 7, 1862, *ibid.,* Ser. IV, Vol. I, pp. 977–980.

[37] The story of Adams' removal and the problem of funds is developed more fully in Chapter VI.

[38] *Texas Almanac—Extra,* November 1, 1862.

chief source of clothing for Texas troops in the Trans-Mississippi.[39]

Texas troops serving in the Tennessee theater also sent wagons for clothing all the way to their home counties in Texas. In a letter to his sweetheart in October, 1862, Private Andrew J. Fogle of Company C of Young's Regiment, Ector's Brigade, wrote from the Knoxville area that his first sergeant and another man were leaving with wagons for the Sherman, Texas, area to get clothing. Fogle seemed more interested at the time in receiving a letter from the girl via these wagons than in any clothes she might send him. Four months later he reported the return of the clothing detail from Texas, and he was delighted to find a letter from his correspondent folded in one of the garments.[40] This four-month trip may not be a record for sustained effort, but it illustrates the determination of some devoted combat men to keep themselves in the field when official resources failed.

Semblance of Order: Appearance of the Clothing Bureau

Some semblance of regional coordination and planning became possible in the midsummer of 1862 when Holmes finally directed one of his quartermasters, Major John B. Burton, later called by the *Washington* (Arkansas) *Telegraph* an "efficient" and "affable" officer, to set up a departmental Clothing Bureau.[41] By the end of the summer Burton was ready to publish his plans in most departmental newspapers. He announced that agents had been appointed and depots established throughout Holmes' command. The chief agent for southern Texas and New Mexico operated from San Antonio, while the chief agent for northern Texas was based at Jefferson. All agencies previously concerned with clothing and equipage supply were either to work with these two men in their respective areas, or were to consider themselves "annulled," as Burton phrased it. All

---

[39] O. M. Roberts, "Texas," in *Confederate Military History, a Library of Confederate States History* (Clement A. Evans, ed.), XI, 114.

[40] Fogle to Louisa Harris, October 29, 1862; March 31, 1863. Andrew J. Fogle Papers, Archives of The University of Texas Library.

[41] Special Orders No. 164, Adjutant and Inspector General's Office, Richmond, July 16, 1862, *Official Records,* Ser. I, Vol. XIII, p. 855; Directive of Major General Holmes, *Dallas Herald,* December 6, 1862; *Washington Telegraph* (Arkansas) March 11, 1863.

agents south of Huntsville reported to San Antonio; those north reported to Jefferson. Agent reports showed work done, in progress, and in prospect. Burton believed his plan would "effect a system, which [would] fully develop the resources of the State—give encouragement to 'home industry,' and make the Military Department, as to clothing its soldiers, self-sustaining." [42] While Burton's arrangements were being developed, Holmes' "acting chief quartermaster," Captain John D. Adams, at Holmes' direction, exhorted the public to greater effort in home manufacture. Finished products could be delivered to local county clerks, who would forward them to the nearest post quartermaster.

Although the Bureau plans met with general approval throughout the Department, at least one skeptical sneer appeared in prominent print:

The great Clothing Beaureau [sic] intended to be established by the C. Government, and about which so much has been said, is now receiving some attention from the officers appointed to that duty. If the war continues *long enough,* it doubtless will be perfect in all its details. [43]

Burton's Bureau was now organized and directives published, but critical shortages still existed in the early winter of 1862. Faced with urgent want, Generals Richard Taylor and Holmes in November pirated a large shipment of cloth ticketed for the eastern theater. The consignment had arrived in Taylor's district at Alexandria, Louisiana, unaccompanied by the officer in charge of the goods. Taylor distributed some of the material to his troops, ordering his chief quartermaster to have civilians make it up into uniforms. Holmes, hearing of Taylor's action, ordered the remainder of the shipment to Little Rock. The affair greatly annoyed Quartermaster General Myers, as being "one of numerous instances in which department commanders assume to exercise authority over subjects the responsibility for and control of which belong exclusively to the department." [44]

[42] *Washington Telegraph,* September 3, 1862.
[43] *Texas Almanac—Extra,* December 23, 1862.
[44] Taylor to Cooper, November 21, 1862, *Official Records,* Ser. I, Vol. XV, p. 872; Myers' endorsement to Randolph, December 8, 1862, *ibid.*

Except for this anecdote of friction between Richmond and Western commanders, sources say little of efforts to obtain clothing in the winter of 1862–1863. There was growing concern over speculation among private interests which dealt in hides and leather, and officials of the Bureau moved in February to stop the evil by tightening control over the supply of hides.[45] A new chief of bureau, Major W. H. Haynes, began his regime in Little Rock with a circular on February 17, 1863, directing post quartermasters to cope with speculation among leather and shoe producers. Since the government controlled the hide supply, prices could be held down to a dollar per pair for shoes. "The Qr Master Dept should put down so far as in its power, the extortioners." By the end of the year the Clothing Bureau was in operation, but an objective evaluation of its success must await reports growing out of grander operations in 1863 under the administration of its new chief, Major W. H. Haynes.

Bureau Operations, 1863

On March 7, 1863, General Kirby-Smith assumed command of the entire Trans-Mississippi Department; General Holmes was retained as commander of the Arkansas District.[46] In Kirby-Smith's opinion Holmes never had given serious attention to anything south of Arkansas. As a consequence, Smith reported, "There was no general system, no common head; each district was acting independently." It was necessary, Smith believed, to "begin *de novo* in any attempt at a general systematizing and development of the departmental resources." [47] All departmental bureau offices must now be moved closer to headquarters. Consequently, Major W. H. Haynes, Smith's appointee, directed clothing operations from Shreveport after June 15, 1863.[48]

---

[45] Circular in Birge Papers, Case 14.
[46] General Orders Nos. 1–8, *General Orders, Trans-Mississippi Department*, pp. 1–3.
[47] Joseph Howard Parks, *General Edmund Kirby Smith, C.S.A.*, pp. 257–258; Kirby-Smith to Jefferson Davis, June 16, 1863, *Official Records*, Ser. I, Vol. XXII, Pt. II, pp. 871–873.
[48] General Orders No. 19, *General Orders, Trans-Mississippi Department*, p. 13.

In order to get a picture of his departmental inventory, present and future, Haynes opened office with orders to all clothing officers and agents to report on six matters: (1) inventory on hand, (2) contracts out and status of each, (3) depot and local prospects of manufacture, (4) location and capacity of factories, shops, and tanneries, (5) location and boundaries of officer's or agent's district, (6) account of all employed personnel, specifying exact duties and pay of each.[49] On October 14 Haynes published an appeal to private manufacturers and the ladies' groups to work even harder to supply their favorite troops. He promised to pay for all such manufactures at the quartermaster depot closest to the establishment of the maker or supplier; he further promised to send such articles to the men of the command for whom they were intended unless these men had been already supplied, in which case the issue would be made "to others who may be in want."[50]

While Major Haynes tried to extend operations into all parts of the Trans-Mississippi, General Magruder seemingly took steps in Texas to set up his own clothing bureau without regard for the Shreveport office. Major E. C. Wharton, assistant to Major Benjamin Bloomfield, Magruder's quartermaster, headed this Texas bureau, directing activities of three subdistrict depot quartermasters, under whom all agents were to operate.

Haynes did not learn of the Texas organization, apparently, until he arrived in Houston to brief Bloomfield on the grander plan. Faced with the semiaccomplished fact, Haynes endorsed Wharton's arrangements, requesting that the subdistrict depots be at Tyler, for the Northern Subdistrict; at San Antonio, for the Western Subdistrict; and at Houston, for the Eastern Subdistrict.[51] Although Magruder necessarily, at the time, acknowledged Haynes' authority

---

[49] Circular, June 18, 1863, *Arkansas Patriot,* July 4, 1863. An important Bureau agent at this period of the war was John Henry Brown, who advertised actively for clothing in central Texas in the spring of 1863. Brown promised "cash." *The Texas Almanac—Extra,* April 2, 1863.

[50] Circular in *Southwestern* (Shreveport, Louisiana), October 14, 1863.

[51] The three subdistrict boundaries were defined by a general order on June 23, 1863, General Orders No. 97, Headquarters, District of Texas, New Mexico, and Arizona, *Official Records,* Ser. I, Vol. XXVI, Pt. II, p. 80.

over stock control,[52] he evidently requisitioned directly from Wharton without clearing through Shreveport. Wharton thus fretted into the fall over having two "bosses," either of whom could alter his clothing stock without referring to the other. He understood that he was somehow semi-independent of Haynes: he could import directly from Rio Grande sources. But the respectable resources of the Texas Penitentiary came under Haynes' control. Haynes left supply of troops in Texas to Wharton while giving personal attention to supplying troops on duty in Arkansas and Louisiana.[53] In October, General Kirby-Smith's inspector general, after a tour of troop sites, declared a number of units in Arkansas and the Indian Territory to be poorly clad while other companies were in good shape. There was "inequality in the distribution of clothing," which might have been unavoidable, but why it existed at all the inspector general could not understand.[54]

Indian leaders had complained repeatedly since the first campaigns that Confederate supply services neglected them. In February, 1862, when a shipment of uniforms intended for the Indians arrived at the field depot of General Sterling Price, the entire shipment was appropriated for Price's men. The poet general and Indian agent, Albert Pike, was furious over the piracy. As Frank Cunningham describes the result, Stand Watie's able Cherokees "remained in odd shirts and pants, moccasins and hats with feathers sticking in them." [55]

Stand Watie, himself, in an appeal to Richmond in August, 1862, explained with dignity that clothing "procured at great trouble and expense, to cover the nakedness of Indian troops, has on several occasions been distributed among less necessitous soldiers." He ac-

[52] Wharton to Turner, October 12, 1863, *ibid.,* pp. 305–308.
[53] *Ibid.,* p. 308.
[54] Schaumburg to Boggs, October 26, 1863, *Official Records,* Ser. I, Vol. XXII, Pt. II, pp. 1049–1053. Lieutenant Colonel Arthur Fremantle, the British traveler and observer, noted at Monroe, Louisiana, in May, 1863, that while men of General Walker's division were well armed with rifles and bayonets, "they were dressed in ragged civilian clothes." Walter Lord (ed.), *The Fremantle Diary: Being the Journal of Lieutenant Colonel James Arthur Lyon Fremantle, Coldstream Guards, or His Three Months in the Southern States,* p. 69.
[55] Cunningham, *General Stand Watie's Confederate Indians,* p. 54.

knowledged, however, that of late his command had been "better provided for than formerly." [56] The array of problems in this complex command, the Indian Territory, completely defeated Confederate General William Steele who struggled throughout 1863 with what he called, in a word, "chaos" in his isolated province. Following his relief from the nightmare, Steele sat down in Galveston and sought to explain in organized detail why the Territory command problem had become so hopeless:

I was fully and truthfully advised by Major-General Hindman of the exhausted condition of the country, as well as the undisciplined, ill-equipped, and demoralized state of the few troops over whom I was called to command. . . . The quartermaster and commissary departments throughout the Territory were found in utmost confusion.[57]

The disgruntled Steele, chafing from remarks about his failure and insinuations about his Yankee origins, declared that most of his staff officers had been incompetent and negligent appointees of Generals Hindman and Pike. Consequently, he said, he had never received "a single paper . . . in the way of a record, either in reference to previous military operations or the Indian superintendency." The Indians, equipped or not, Steele believed, with few exceptions, to be wholly unreliable as troops of the line.[58] Steele's judgment was too harsh; the Indians, it should be said, continued to keep an effective force in the field, thwarting Federal plans in the area, especially under Watie, until after the surrender of the Trans-Mississippi Department in 1865.

The unfavorable report of his inspector general on clothing conditions among the Indians and in Arkansas, coupled with differences between Wharton and Haynes, probably caused General Kirby-Smith in mid-November to establish a standard allocation of imported clothing, camp or garrison equipage: four-tenths to the depots at Bonham and Jefferson for the use of Arkansas and Indian Territory troops; two-tenths to San Antonio and Houston for General Magruder's command (excepting McCulloch's, which was sup-

[56] *Ibid.,* p. 103.
[57] *Ibid.,* p. 119.
[58] *Ibid.*

plied from Bonham); three-tenths to Shreveport for the District of Western Louisiana; and one-tenth to Major Haynes' general depot for the troops-at-large.[59]

Soon after the establishment of these allocations the War Department ordered a full inspection of the Trans-Mississippi Department by Major J. P. Johnson, adjutant and inspector general. From Richmond, Johnson came to look over carefully every administrative detail in "Kirby Smithdom." Surprisingly, perhaps, the Quartermaster's Department survived rather well the rigors of Johnson's inspection. He found the corps satisfactorily organized and competent and systematic in keeping accounts and funds. The troops were "tolerably well clothed" and the transportation on hand was ample and in good condition.[60] That same season a grand jury investigated charges of fraud in the supply services in the "Eastern District of Texas" without uncovering any wrongdoing. One member of the jury, at least, reported to the press that he was of the opinion that discrepancies in the accounts were just too "well cloaked." [61]

Inspector Johnson's visit, since it stirred Haynes to compile a hasty report of Clothing Bureau operations as of the beginning of 1864,[62] was a propitious event for the student of Confederate supply arrangements. Arrangements had been made for the monthly delivery to depots at Tyler, Jefferson, or Shreveport of 9,000 to 13,000 hats, at a cost of $3.25 to $5.00 each. In shoe shops at Shreveport, Washington (Arkansas), Jefferson, Tyler, Houston, and Austin, about 10,000 pairs of shoes were manufactured per month. The Texas Penitentiary at Huntsville intended to supply 1,200,000 yards of cloth, Osnaburg, cotton jeans, and woolen plaids and jeans during 1864. The financial agent of the Penitentiary reported that the plant had produced 1,419,364½ yards of cotton goods and 292,-963½ yards of woolens for the Confederate forces between Decem-

[59] General Orders No. 56, *General Orders of the Trans-Mississippi Department,* p. 36.

[60] "Consolidated inspection report of Trans-Mississippi Department, made by order of the Adjutant and Inspector General of the Confederate States Army," February 16, 1864, *Official Records,* Ser. I, Vol. XXII, Pt. II, p. 1128.

[61] *Galveston Tri-Weekly News,* July 18, 1864.

[62] Haynes to Boggs, January 11, 1864, *Official Records,* Ser. I, Vol. XXII, Pt. II, p. 1136.

ber 1, 1861, and December 18, 1863.[63] Governor Lubbock stated in February, 1863, that he had not renewed a contract made by his predecessor in 1861 with Confederate agents in Tennessee to supply one-half of the output of the Huntsville machinery to that theater. The Tennessee contract was allowed to expire in April, 1862, Lubbock said, when he failed to receive assurances that the Penitentiary product was going to Texas troops. Subsequent state policy supplied Texas soldiers first, and then their families, and, finally, nonspeculative consumers. "It has been found that our soldiers have received three-fourths of the woolen goods and over half of the cotton goods." All woolen goods were to go to the Army henceforth, Lubbock concluded.[64]

Haynes' report of issues during the year ending December 31, 1863, provides opportunity for evaluation of his efforts to that date: [65]

Item	Total Amount	Amount of Total Manufactured by the Bureau
Caps and hats	19,732	15,230
Jackets	25,557	7,657
Pants, prs.	41,157	21,747
Overshirts	2,210	139
Shirts	54,585	43,651
Drawers, prs.	48,704	38,952
Boots and shoes, prs.	40,860	6,269

Continued on page 36

[63] Haynes to Boggs, January 18, 1864, *ibid.,* p. 1134; report of John S. Besser, financial agent, Texas Penitentiary, *Galveston Tri-Weekly News,* February 1, 1864. Increasing demands from indigent families and other obligations of the state apparently reduced the rate of output to the Confederate Army during 1864. Felgar, "Texas in the War for Southern Independence" (unpublished Ph.D. dissertation), p. 405.

[64] *Galveston Tri-Weekly News,* February 11, 1863.

[65] Haynes to Boggs, January 11, 1864, *Official Records,* Ser. I, Vol. XXII, Pt. II, p. 1136. An example of the use of the Penitentiary source appears in the letterbook of Lieutenant Colonel G. H. Hill of the Tyler Ordnance Works. On September 3, 1864, with the approval of Governor Murrah and Major Haynes, Hill sent wagons to Huntsville to pick up 1,656 yards of Osnaburg to be made into clothing for his men and employees. "Letters sent by Lieutenant Colonel G. H. Hill, Commander of the Confederate Ordnance Works at Tyler, Texas, 1864–1865," Record Group 109, Chap. IV, Vol. 147, National Archives, Washington, D.C. Hereafter referred to as Hill Letterbook.

Item	Total Amount	Amount of Total Manufactured by the Bureau
Socks, prs.	5,356	
Overcoats	637	571
Blankets and quilts	22,236	311
Alpaca, yds.	300⅛	
Cassimere, yds.	140½	
Cloth, gray, yds.	12,473	
Cottonade, yds.	444½	
Domestic, yds.	30,521½	
Drilling, yds.	96¾	
Flannel, yds.	671¼	
Jeans, yds.	4,675¾	302¼
Jeans, cotton	1,390¼	
Kersey, yds.	711½	
Linsey, yds.	105½	26¼
Leather, harness, lbs.	5,295	5,609
Leather, sole, lbs.	1,027¾	
Leather, lbs.	14,865	
Leather, upper, lbs.	715	
Osnaburg, yds.	2,966	
Tweed, yds.	24½	
Wool, lbs.	41,532	
Wool, rolls, lbs.	706	
Knapsacks	1,714	1,372
Haversacks	9,010	9,162
Tent flies	332	216
"A" tents	610	546
Wall tents	443	202
Wagonsheets	595	590

The above figures have little significance if they are not considered in the light of the number of troops in the area which Haynes presumed to supply. The return for the Districts of Arkansas, Indian Territory, and West Louisiana indicated an aggregate (present and absent) of 54,254 enlisted men at the close of 1863.[66] Of these, only 22,676 were actually present for duty. Where the remainder were is

[66] Haynes to Boggs, January 11, 1864, *Official Records,* Ser. I, Vol. XXII, Pt. II, p. 1127.

a matter for interesting speculation, but the fluctuation of personnel would possibly have brought almost all of the aggregate number of these men into the present-for-duty status during the course of the year, thus necessitating supplying them with clothing. In such an event, the Bureau would have been short approximately 14,000 pairs of shoes if only one issue were required; undoubtedly several issues were necessary for each man because of the lengthy marches required during the campaigning in that area. Reference to the foregoing list reveals that for no single item was there nearly a sufficient supply for 54,000 troops, based on the official authorization of clothing. Particularly inadequate was the number of overcoats (only 637) handled by the Bureau. Another factor which experienced supply people will recognize as significant in creating shortages is that combat and hard-marching troops tend to discard equipment. The historian of the Federal quartermaster service quotes the unhappy General Meigs on this point:

"Knapsacks are piled, blankets, overcoats, and other clothing thrown off, and whether victorious or defeated, the regiments seem seldom to recover the property thus laid aside." As might have been expected, volunteers were more wasteful than regulars. Appropriations for clothing and equipment for the volunteer army based on allowances for the regular army fell short of the mark.[67]

Bureau Operations, 1864–1865

In June, 1864, Haynes presented a comprehensive, carefully considered estimate of the supply situation for the year 1864–1865. Bureau output remained totally inadequate, but Haynes was convinced the fault lay outside the province of his officers:

Having made known my wants to the proper officials by timely requisitions—having to some extent employed the odious contract system, against which too much cannot be said—it is a painful reflection to know that my sanguine anticipations have not been realized. The failure of the accredited purchasing officers; the fall of Brownsville, losing thereby large supplies which could have been secured in the summer of 1863; fall

[67] Weigley, *Quartermaster General of the Union Army*, p. 254.

of Vicksburg and the interruption of intercourse, thereby preventing the passage of clothing to this department which had been secured by my agents; the depreciation of the currency and consequent interference in purchasing some fabrics, and many other causes have conduced to the paralyzation of the operation of this bureau.[68]

There were plenty of raw materials in the Trans-Mississippi, Haynes pointed out, but insufficient means for converting them into finished products. Nevertheless, he expressed hopes for 1865, by which time several contemplated clothing and equipage factories would relieve the Army of such heavy recourse to importations. But until these "resources" were available, dependence would still have to be on the handlooms of the country, the products of the Texas Penitentiary, the purchases of the departmental Cotton Bureau, and on the purchases of Major Simeon Hart, the general purchasing agent of the War Department.

Haynes blamed Major Hart for failing to meet requisitions made on him in 1863. A major requisition for 30,000 "outfits," approved by the quartermaster general in April, 1863, had never been filled. Haynes doubted that Hart had even been able to supply the Western Subdistrict of Texas.[69] He would have been bemused, probably, had he known how well garbed were some of the troops in the Western Subdistrict. Colonel Fremantle believed the 3rd Texas Infantry, of General Bee's command, to be the best-dressed and best-drilled regiment he saw in his entire tour of the South in 1863.[70]

After the Red River Campaign in the spring of 1864, Haynes got caught up in the explosive exchange of notes between Generals Kirby-Smith and Dick Taylor. Sick and bitter in his disappointment at being unable to finish off the Federal general, Banks, Taylor lashed out venomously at everything he could associate with Smith's system of operation. Quartermaster supply inevitably became a peripheral target for Taylor's scorn. Taylor believed that Smith should have combined forces against Banks instead of dissipating strength

[68] Haynes to Boggs, June 10, 1864, *Official Records,* Ser. I, Vol. XXXIV, Pt. IV, p. 657.
[69] *Ibid.,* p. 657.
[70] Lord (ed.), *Fremantle Diary,* p. 16 and p. 16 n.

by galloping off against Steele in Arkansas. The "game" (Banks and Porter) had been allowed to escape through Kirby-Smith's "pitiably wrong" policy was Taylor's emphatic conclusion.[71] Soon after his return from Arkansas in May, Kirby-Smith received a second diatribe from Taylor, complaining that his ranks had thinned away because of supply failures. Shoe shortages, despite "liberal" Clothing Bureau promises, continued while Haynes' agents remained "barren in performance." "No campaign dependent on the present system of bureaucracy" would succeed, said Taylor. "The rage" for "organization" had gone so far that the result was like a "disproportioned garment—all ruffles and no shirt." [72] The conscript laws were a delusion, he continued; details of men for noncombat duty daily cut deeper into the limited supply of veteran soldiers, and while the Army lacked food, clothing, and pay, requisitions remained lost in a "mingled maze of red tape and circumlocution." [73]

Taylor's charges brought a prompt itemized counter from Kirby-Smith: the indictment of the Conscript Bureau was possible only because of Taylor's failure to support its efforts in his command. In Smith's view, the Clothing Bureau had done well despite being "crippled in its resources and cut off from its supplies by the loss of the Rio Grande and the actions of the Governor of Texas and its State Legislature." This last reference was directed at Governor Pendleton Murrah who had set up a Military Board which competed with Confederate purchasing agents.[74] Despite these handicaps Kirby-Smith insisted to Taylor that his supply officers reported adequate funds and supplies on hand to take care of all Louisiana troops.[75] The generals' feud ended, temporarily, in bitterness, with Taylor assigned east of the Mississippi.

[71] Taylor to Kirby-Smith, April 28, 1864, *Official Records,* Ser. I, Vol. XXXIV, Pt. I, pp. 541–543.

[72] Taylor to Kirby-Smith, May 24, 1864, *ibid.,* Ser. I, Vol. XXXIV, Pt. I, pp. 543–545.

[73] *Ibid.*

[74] Kirby-Smith to Taylor, June 5, 1864, *Official Records,* Ser. I, Vol. XXXIV, Pt. I, p. 539; C. W. Ramsdell, "The Texas State Military Board, 1862–1865," *Southwestern Historical Quarterly,* XXVII (April, 1924), 253–275.

[75] Kirby-Smith to Taylor, June 5, 1864, *Official Records,* Ser. I, Vol. XXXIV, Pt. I, pp. 538–540.

Although Shreveport and Marshall supply reports may have temporarily supported Smith's assertion of material and financial competence in the summer of 1864, matters worsened rapidly in the early fall. As Major Haynes had predicted, the Clothing Bureau fell far short of providing necessities for what proved to be the last winter of the war. As early as August 10, 1864, Major General S. B. Maxey published a clothing appeal in the *Dallas Herald*. Home folks of each regiment again were asked to concentrate contributions in specified towns. Maxey arranged transportation to carry the supplies to his men in the field in Oklahoma Territory.[76] Maxey's disillusioned chaplain seconded the General's appeal, remarking that after "many fair promises during the past summer, of vast amounts of clothing being procured by the Qr. Masters, the melancholy information is forced upon us that their efforts have proved abortive and their promises delusive." [77] Response from the home folks was good, however, and November 20, 1864, found the Lane Rangers in Arkansas decked out in new garb on the Sabbath. Their historian, W. W. Heartsill, reported: "No one would recognize the 'W. P. Lane Rangers' of today, as the 'Ragamuffins' of yesterday: very near every man has nice new clothing, but there are a few however who have no kind relatives in the house of their adoption to remember them so generously." [78] Appeals "to the people" continued to appear in the Texas press in September and October.[79] Other newspaper comment criticized as inelastic the percentage allocation system which had been in operation since 1863. Soldiers on furlough from Arkansas and Louisiana complained that when they arrived in Houston, they could not draw clothing which they needed because of the district allocation system but that the noncombatant soldiers of the Cotton Office at Houston seemed to be well dressed.[80]

Perhaps because of such comment on Bureau failure to provide fully for all the troops, in December Kirby-Smith placed Bureau

---

[76] *Dallas Herald*, August 27, 1864.

[77] *Ibid.*, September 10, 1864.

[78] Heartsill, *Fourteen Hundred and 91 Days*, p. 223.

[79] Examples were *Galveston Tri-Weekly News*, September 19, October 3 and October 26, 1864.

[80] *Galveston Tri-Weekly News*, December 28, 1864.

officers and personnel directly under control of the chief quarter-master, Captain John E. Garey.[81] By virtue of his position on Kirby-Smith's staff, Garey thus ranked quartermasters bearing grades of major and lieutenant colonel. Shreveport, Houston, and Bonham were announced as general depots for the supply of all quartermaster items. All requisitions on these centers must clear through District quartermaster offices en route to Garey, who would finally decide on priority of issues. All quartermaster property coming from abroad was directed to these three depots. All Clothing Bureau manufactures in the future would be delivered on Garey's personal order. The chain of command in this new and final system functioned as follows: Garey sent approved requisitions and other directives to Lieutenant Colonel L. W. O'Bannon, chief of the Quartermaster's Bureau in Marshall, who then directed Major Haynes to deliver as specified.[82]

General Kirby-Smith might now be better able to fix responsibility for issues and allocations, but no amount of bureaus or chains of command through bureaus and across desk tops was adequate to solve the supply problem in 1865. Financial demoralization in the last year had proved ruinous to best-laid plans, and by the close of 1864, unpaid civilian claims attained the level of $40 million for supplies and services rendered Confederate authorities. Major Haynes noted that nearly every farmer bore some of the "promises to pay" (certified accounts) and did not wish any more of them. In despair Haynes concluded in a report to Kirby-Smith on Department prospects: "We cannot use certified accounts, cannot use the large size certificates of indebtedness; cannot impress; have no currency; the army is in want; it cannot be supplied." [83] Smith forwarded Haynes' remarks to Richmond, at the same time

---

[81] General Orders No. 94, December 3, 1864, *General Orders of the Trans-Mississippi Department*, p. 83. Captain Garey had been appointed chief quartermaster on June 23, 1864, by General Orders No. 49, *ibid.*, p. 48. Actually, the bulk of all quartermaster paper-work was handled by Lieutenant Colonel O'Bannon's Bureau, which had its office at Marshall, Texas. *Ibid.*, p. 25.

[82] *Ibid.*

[83] Haynes to Boggs, February 8, 1865, *Official Records*, Ser. I, Vol. XLVIII, Pt. I, pp. 1382–1383.

urging the return shipment of $30 million or $40 million. Copies of Haynes' letter went also to Texas Senators L. T. Wigfall and W. S. Oldham with an urgent plea for congressional help on the financial problem. Judge P. W. Gray, treasury agent for the Trans-Mississippi Department, responding to Haynes' report, agreed that the picture was hopeless. The Treasury had no funds, Gray lacked authority to arrange even a temporary loan, and little help would or could come from Richmond.[84]

The quartermasters' quest had failed to find a remedy for continuing shortages of clothing and camp and garrison equipage. Although reports of inspectors general, like those of other governmental investigations, are not necessarily infallible, they do in this account support the conclusion that the Trans-Mississippi quartermaster on occasion came close to success.[85] Explanations for lack of success should ever include the reminder that the South was totally unprepared for the task of equipping armies for the field in several theaters. It had few factories for processing available raw materials. An organization for exploiting limited resources had to be developed from vague, unsteady origins; there was no other way because the general plan of the government during the first year was for a short war and short-term supply arrangements. When it was realized that the war was to be lengthy, the quartermaster began long-term planning, but almost every factor which contributed to the collapse of the Confederacy operated to impair progress of any plans. Cut off from the east, the Trans-Mississippi quartermaster had to depend upon the people of the area and upon general purchasing agents. Major Haynes blamed the failure of these agents, the isolation of the Department, and the unstable status of Confederate finances for his inadequacies.

[84] Smith to Seddon, February 11, 1865, *ibid.*, pp. 1381–1382; Smith to Gray, February 11, 1865, *ibid.*, pp. 1383–1384; Gray to Smith, February 24, 1865, *ibid.*, pp. 1401–1402.

[85] In his study of Texas in the war, Robert P. Felgar concluded that although Texas troops in other theaters suffered from want of hospital supplies, shoes, and clothing, those in the Trans-Mississippi Department "were reasonably well supplied with shoes and clothing." See Felgar, "Texas in the War for Southern Independence" (unpublished Ph.D. dissertation), p. 425.

III

The Tax-in-Kind in the Trans-Mississippi

Passage of the tax-in-kind act on April 24, 1863, required the heavily laden Quartermaster's Department to assemble a sub-bureau mechanism of special post quartermasters.[1] From Richmond, Colonel Larkin Smith, assistant quartermaster general, provided direction to a network which included one post quartermaster for each congressional district and one controlling quartermaster for each state.[2]

In the Trans-Mississippi area General Kirby-Smith's batch of bureaus at Marshall, Texas, was thus increased by one; that is, because of isolation from Richmond, a central coordinating office was needed to direct post and state controlling officers authorized by the tithe act.[3] Head of the new bureau was Major Benjamin A. Botts, whose letterbook affords a day-by-day chronicle of tax-in-kind operations in the Trans-Mississippi.[4]

[1] Portions of this chapter appeared in *Civil War History,* V (December, 1959), 382–389.

[2] Lester and Bromwell, *Digest of the Military and Naval Laws,* pp. 177–179, 181. A list of officers, agents, and men assigned to the collection of the tax-in-kind is included in Chap. V, Vol. 199, Record Group 109 in the National Archives (microfilm copy in possession of the writer).

[3] Public attention to the tithe act was asked in Trans-Mississippi press notices in the late summer. An example is in the *Washington Telegraph* for August 5, 1863.

[4] Benjamin A. Botts Letterbook. Hereafter cited as Botts Letterbook.

The tithe act specifically affected crops of oats, rye, buckwheat, rice, sweet and Irish potatoes, cured hay and fodder, sugar, molasses, cotton, wool, and tobacco. The tax, however, would not operate to deny a farm family of a necessary reserve of rations. With livestock added to the list, producers in the Trans-Mississippi were told to prepare one-tenth of the meat for the government (hog meat at the ratio of 60 pounds of cured bacon to each 100 pounds of pork).

Local tax assessors estimated each prospective crop and informed the producer of the estimate.[5] If the producer thought the evaluation too high, he and the assessor called in a third party, a freeholder, and, if necessary, a fourth party joined the conference. When appraisers agreed, the final crop estimate was written out in duplicate, the original to the assessor and the copy to the producer. Tax assessors sent copies of their estimates to the post quartermaster, who receipted for them.[6] These receipts, in the Trans-Mississippi, came finally to the hands of the departmental auditor, who could then check the accountability of each quartermaster. Each producer was required to deliver, within sixty days after his assessment, his tax in "marketable" condition to a depot located not more than eight miles from his collecting point. The government paid transportation costs for distances of more than eight miles and agreed to furnish grain sacks and to make allowance for the cost of molasses barrels. Failure to deliver within the prescribed period brought a penalty of 50 per cent of the tithe, making a total obligation of 15 per cent of the crop. If the producer defaulted completely, the post quartermaster notified the district tax collector, who issued a distress warrant for the sale of the producer's property in order to collect the tax.

Having received the assessment against a producer's crop, the

---

[5] An example of an estimate against the 1865 crop of a Nacogdoches, Texas, planter, indicating a tithe of 142 bushels of corn, valued at $355, appears in the Bennett Blake Papers, hereafter cited as Blake Papers.

[6] Copies of all forms used, along with complete tax-in-kind instructions, were published in a booklet, a copy of which is preserved in Chap. V, Vols. 199 and 199½, Record Group 109, National Archives.

post quartermaster was responsible for collection and storage of the tithe until it was taken for uses of the Army or Treasury department. Later amendments permitted growers to keep all corn under 200 bushels, to substitute salt pork for cured bacon, and to receive credit for losses due to enemy action or accident. General revision of the tax act on February 17, 1864, brought a number of exemptions for families of meager means.[7]

As the tithe flowed in through his scattered depots, the post quartermaster set aside the cotton, wool, and tobacco for treasury agents, who receipted to him and removed such produce to their storage points. Forage and subsistence items were placed where they could be used practicably by the Army. In locales where collection in kind was impracticable, a commuted value in money was accepted for treasury account. Quartermasters in charge could sell produce endangered either by spoilage or enemy activity.

The Army undoubtedly felt the benefits of the act at once; here was a method for quick procurement of forage and subsistence. Previously the purchasing commissaries and depot and field quartermasters had had to persuade reluctant producers to accept Confederate cash at Army prices. Frequently, supply officers had to resort to the hateful impressment device. Whether the tax-in-kind was to be less hateful remained to be seen.

By October 10, 1863, Trans-Mississippi tax-in-kind machinery consisted of three state controlling quartermasters—over Texas, Arkansas, and Louisiana, respectively—and an array of post quartermasters with their county agents, subagents, wagons, and teamsters.[8]

A typical post quartermaster was Captain George C. Rives, assigned on August 24, 1863, to the Second Congressional District of Texas. Rives' papers, apparently complete, offer a "grass roots"

[7] Lester and Bromwell, *Digest of the Military and Naval Laws of the Confederate States,* pp. 178, 182–184.

[8] *Bellville Countryman,* October 10, 1863; Botts Letterbook. At least, this system existed on paper. Captain J. W. Sims, post quartermaster at Natchitoches, Louisiana, reflected some confusion as to his duties in the system in a letter to departmental headquarters on November 9, 1863. Letterbook of Captain J. W. Sims, in the J. Fair Hardin Collection. Hereafter cited as Sims Letterbook.

supplement to Major Botts' higher-echelon activities.[9] From his office in Austin, Rives guided tithe affairs in a tremendous district embracing eighteen counties. In each of these counties Rives appointed a county agent, who, where necessary, employed subagents as custodians of subdepots.

Rives' first concern was to line up a supply of grain sacks to receive the 1863 tithe. His superior at Nacogdoches, James R. Arnold, controlling quartermaster for Texas, anticipated the problem by arranging a contract with John S. Besser, financial agent of the Texas Penitentiary, for the manufacture of 50,000 yards of Osnaburg cloth, of which 6,000 yards would go to Rives on November 28. The Penitentiary supplied thread for the sewing process.[10] By November 9 Arnold and Rives had begun to fret over the slowness of the assessors in completing the appraisal. Arnold feared that winter rains and impassable roads would prevent effective collection and distribution of the produce to troops who needed it immediately.[11]

Some of the needy troops in Texas, Rives soon learned, had already, on their own initiative, begun to pick up the tithe before the arrival of regular collectors. Agents at Columbus and in Wharton County reported that farmers were delivering produce on demand to any passing officer or "others in charge of government trains." For the post quartermaster to obtain vouchers from these transient consumers was practically impossible.[12]

---

[9] Portfolio of correspondence of Captain George C. Rives in Miscellaneous Records of the Quartermaster and Commissary Departments for the State of Texas and the Confederate States, 1861–1865, hereafter cited as Rives Correspondence. The letterbook of Captain J. W. Sims, cited in the previous note, provides similar material on the operations of the post quartermaster in northwestern Louisiana. Sims hired several agents at $83.00 per month for tithe collection in mid-November and directed them not to issue produce to "irresponsible persons." Sims to Messrs. Carver, Dempsey, Tucker, Collins, Durham, November 16, 17, 18, 1863, Sims Letterbook.

[10] Arnold to Rives, November 7, 1863, Besser to Rives, November 16, 1863, Rives Correspondence.

[11] Arnold to Rives, November 9, 1863, *ibid.*

[12] Arnold to Rives, February 29, 1864, *ibid.* Tithe officers in Arkansas, having the same problem, warned planters and military personnel in newspaper notices that only tax officers could legally collect and receipt for their produce. *Washington Telegraph,* December 2, 1863.

That the problem of proper vouchers was widespread was indicated by the appearance of General Order No. 48 from the adjutant and inspector general at Richmond, issued in May, 1864.
Military and civilian personnel were firmly reminded that only
bonded quartermasters, commissaries, and Treasury agents could
receipt to producers for the tithe.[13] In August, 1864, Quartermaster
General A. R. Lawton and Commissary General L. B. Northrop
jointly circulated a warning that receipts from other than bonded
officers or agents were worthless.[14] Thereafter, Major Botts promptly
reported every case of violation in the Trans-Mississippi directly to
Kirby-Smith's headquarters and vehemently insisted on disciplinary
action. Failure to stop indiscriminate collection would result, Botts
said, in "the same Waste and Confusion" as had occurred during the
1863 season.[15]

Principal consumers of the tithe in Texas, in addition to regular
and state troops, included the personnel and livestock of the Texas
Cotton Office (see Chapter IV), who were engaged in Kirby-Smith's
extensive Rio Grande convoy system. Major Simeon Hart, controversial predecessor of the Cotton Office, who continued to operate
as a quartermaster purchasing agent, made heavy use of tithe
sources.[16] Soon after Rives assumed accountability, letters of inquiry
and requisitions poured into his office from every kind of officer
wanting forage and subsistence supplies. For example, Lieutenant
R. L. Sprigg, of the Niter and Mining Bureau, in charge of the niter
works in Burnet County, asked and received permission to share
supplies from Lampasas and Burnet Counties with the Texas Frontier Regiment. The recruiting service received authority to draw
freely on tithe sources where troop quartermasters and commissaries
were not available to make arrangements.[17] From Smith County the

---

[13] General Orders issued May 28, 1864, *General Orders from the Adjutant and
Inspector General's Office, Confederate States Army, From January 1, 1864, to
July 1, 1864, Inclusive*, pp. 98–99. The Treasury Department transferred complete
control of the management of the tithe to the War Department in March, 1864.
Richard Cecil Todd, *Confederate Finance*, p. 223 n.
[14] Circular, August 8, 1864, *Official Records*, Ser. IV, Vol. III, pp. 574–575.
[15] Botts to Boggs, November 11, 1864, Botts Letterbook.
[16] Arnold to Rives, January 11, 1864, Rives Correspondence.
[17] Rives to Arnold, March 9, 1864; Arnold to Rives, March 18, 1864, *ibid.*

Tyler Ordnance Works wrote for permission to collect forage directly for munition wagon trains. Lieutenant Colonel G. H. Hill, commanding the Ordnance Works, noting that the local post quartermaster was overworked and short of transportation, wished to avoid the necessity of shipping forage with his trains when there was plenty not yet collected by the tithe agents to be had en route.[18]

Illustrative of the monthly receipts in one county of Captain Rives' district are those reported by Samuel Harris, agent for Jackson County, Texas:

Receipts (1864)

April	May	June	July
Sweet potatoes, 50 bu.	189 bu., 10 lbs.	19½ bu.	
Corn 1,671 bu., 18 lbs.	3,314 bu.	85 bu.	
Fodder 5,361 lbs.	16,235 lbs.	....	
Bacon 2,610 lbs.	2,532 lbs.	178 lbs.	2,683 lbs.
Hay	346 lbs.	....	....
(Issued to nine different officers and commissary agents)	(All issued to T. S. Sutherland, quartermaster and commissary agent)		

By September, Harris' receipts were for almost nothing but cotton: 3,851 pounds in September and 21,898 pounds in November.[19]

Travis County reports of Agent J. L. Wallace afford further illustrations of the scope, size, and detail of local operations. Wallace employed four subagents, three at $75.00 a month, one at $100. Principal issues went to the local quartermaster and manufacturing establishment and to the commissary officer in Austin. In February, 1864, these agencies drew 345 bushels of corn, 11,433 pounds of hay, 3,637 pounds of fodder, and 634 pounds of bacon.[20]

---

[18] Hill to Captain E. M. Bacon, P.Q.M., Marshall, June 9, 1864, and Hill to Captain R. M. Vanzant, P.Q.M., Marshall, November 12, 1864, Hill Letterbook.

[19] Monthly reports in portfolio marked "Tax in Kind, Counties J–Z, 1863–1865," Miscellaneous Records of the Quartermaster and Commissary Departments for the State of Texas and the Confederate States, 1861–1865.

[20] *Ibid.*

Bacon storage became Rives' biggest preservation problem early in 1864—particularly in Caldwell County where 14,000 pounds of surplus bacon piled up in June and July. Much of it spoiled despite urgent efforts by Rives' agents to find consumers.[21]

Subsequently, Rives was to be indirectly censured by Brigadier General Henry E. McCulloch, who reported to Department headquarters that the bacon and wheat collected in Bell County were not being appropriated to army use. Ordered to investigate, Rives certified in December that the entire Bell County tithe had been delivered to authorized officers. If any losses had occurred, he asserted, they had come after the produce had passed from his responsibility.[22]

A list of deliveries by Rives to officers of all services in the third quarter of 1864 fills an eighty-six page report. In round figures the issues of major items for the Second Congressional District totaled as follows: [23]

96,000 bu. of corn	1,800 gals. of molasses
58,000 lbs. of hay	350,000 lbs. of bacon
395,000 lbs. of fodder	165,000 lbs. of cotton
3,900 bu. of wheat	

Loss of civilian agents to the draft became a major problem to Rives, as it was to other supply men, after Confederate enrolling officers began to tighten up on conscription. By September of 1862 men between eighteen and forty-five years of age were covered by the call, but the supply services evidently managed to obtain deferments for some essential employees. After February 17, 1864, however, the quartermaster was ordered to retain only those men of draft age who had medical certificates of disability for active field

[21] Arnold to Rives, March 31, 1864; Lester to Rives, July 29, 1864, Rives Correspondence.

[22] McCulloch to Department Headquarters, Shreveport, October 14, 1864, Botts Letterbook; Rives to Arnold, December 5, 1864, *ibid.*

[23] Abstract M, for Third Quarter, 1864, in portfolio marked "Department of Quartermaster, Tax in Kind, 1863–1865," Miscellaneous Records of the Quartermaster, and Commissary Departments.

service.[24] On April 8 Brigadier General Elkanah Greer, chief of the Conscription Bureau in the Trans-Mississippi, directed that tax-in-kind personnel liable to conscription should clear up their affairs in sixty days; "unfit" men must replace them. Then began a wrangle of correspondence lasting until January, 1865, as post quartermasters sought to have cherished clerks and agents deferred or detailed to them.[25]

Like other Confederate agents, Rives ran into serious financial difficulties in the autumn of 1864. His first reference to the money problem in his correspondence with Arnold occurred in October, when he declared that central Texas people had entirely repudiated the currency. As a consequence, his landlord now demanded $50.00 per month in specie. Since his funds of paper money were worthless, he appealed for permission to impress buildings and other necessities. Each impressment of this type had to be approved by Kirby-Smith's headquarters.[26]

Rives' service days were already numbered, however, and he was relieved in January, 1865, by a long-delayed, or shelved, order of the assistant quartermaster general; his commission, it seems, had never been confirmed by Congress. Botts and Arnold had known since July of Rives' loss of officer status, but they had decided they could not spare him. (Here is another example of the bewildering commissioning and personnel processes of the Confederate government.) After all those months of apparently effective, responsible service, his dismissal was possibly welcome to him but also probably an unhappy disillusionment.[27]

The tithe device undoubtedly simplified Kirby-Smith's supply problem for the 1864 campaigns. Reporting to President Davis on

[24] Lester and Bromwell, *Digest of the Military and Naval Laws,* pp. 57, 58, 67.

[25] General Orders No. 8, Headquarters Bureau of Conscription, April 8, 1864, *Galveston Tri-Weekly News,* April 20, 1864; Rives' orders to agents, April 14, 1864, Rives Correspondence; Sellers to Rives, May 11, 1864, *ibid.;* Botts to Greer, Janury 6, Greer to Botts, January 20, 1865, Botts Letterbook.

[26] Rives to Botts, October 20, 1864, *ibid.;* Boggs to Botts, October 12, 1864, *ibid.*

[27] Smith to Botts, July 29, 1864, *ibid.;* Arnold to Rives, September 23, 1864, Rives Correspondence.

August 21, 1864, Smith credited well-located subsistence and forage depots along the roads in counties between the Texas border and the Red River and between Camden, Arkansas, and Natchitoches, Louisiana, with effective supply of the armies of Generals Taylor and Price during the crucial Red River Campaign.[28] Some of the credit for these locations certainly belongs with Captain J. W. Sims and his agents who had charge of tithe collection in this area.

Beginning late in 1864, numerous planters asked tithe officials to permit exchange of produce in one part of the Department for an equal amount of tithe produce in some other district. Such exchanges were approved by the military when the proffered produce was nearer the troops or in a more convenient location for use than were the items designed for exchange. Care was taken to avoid exchanges tainted with speculative possibilities. Transportation of produce from remote areas was reduced to some degree by this policy.[29]

The new exchange policy met with the hearty approval of supply officers with troops in Arkansas and Louisiana. For example, Major C. B. Moore, quartermaster of Brigadier General T. C. Churchill's brigade, applied successfully in November to draw from agreeable producers in Arkansas.[30]

Noticeably scarce in Trans-Mississippi quartermaster records are references to farmer-planter complaints or to dissatisfaction with either the tax act or with personnel employed in its collection. Such an omission is surprising in view of common generalizations that the tax-in-kind was especially unpopular, was resented bitterly by individualistic farmers, and was responsible for creating a horde of officious and sometimes corrupt draft dodgers and bombproof quartermasters.[31] Botts' journal contains only one reference to a case of

[28] Kirby-Smith to President Davis, August 21, 1864, E. Kirby-Smith Papers, hereafter cited as Kirby-Smith Papers. See Sims Letterbook for correspondence on depots at Pleasant Hill, Mansfield, and Wharton's Depot.

[29] Arnold to Botts, October 11, White to Botts, October 22, Botts to Garey, November 3, Botts to Pritchard, November 11, 1864, Botts Letterbook.

[30] Botts to Garey, November 3, 1864, *ibid.*

[31] No tax is ever joyfully received. Some significant resistance to the tax-in-kind developed in the east in the summer of 1863 among the farmer groups. The *North Carolina Standard* (Raleigh) reported accounts of such opposition in issues

alleged fraud by an agent. George A. Fleet, a detailed soldier serving as subagent at Pleasant Hill, De Soto Parish, Louisiana, was brought under inquiry by the inspector general for not reporting all of his collections. For the sake of morale, Botts ordered the man relieved even if found innocent.[32] With the exception of the Fleet case and the McCulloch charges mentioned earlier, the Trans-Mississippi tithe bureau appears to have been relatively free of that type of criticism.

It is apparently impossible to say how much produce was actually derived from the tithe act either in the Trans-Mississippi Department or in the Confederacy as a whole. Richmond authorities estimated the value for the whole Confederacy, by November, 1864, at $150 million.[33] Other appraisers, considerably more conservative, have valued the tithe, to Appomattox, at $145 million. Alexander H. Stephens, ever skeptical of Richmond reports, doubted if more than $40 million worth of goods reached its "proper destination." Whatever the amount, another Georgian, Benjamin H. Hill, believed the tax had averted starvation in the Army.[34] The 1863 gross would have rationed bread and bacon for approximately 160,000 men for one year, had it all been delivered on time and in place—logistical gymnastics beyond the realm of Confederate accomplishment. Results in 1864, hinged as they were to the months of twilight collapse, are understandably even less clear.

One may reasonably conclude, however, that in the Trans-Mississippi Department the troops were comparatively well fed despite financial collapse, transportation slowdown, and tax-in-kind personnel problems.

---

of August 25, 26, and September 1, 1863. These meetings produced resolutions denouncing the tax as unfair when compared with that on salaried classes. Todd, *Confederate Finance,* pp. 142, 223 n.

[32] Trumbull to Botts, October 9, J. P. Smith to Botts, October 19, Botts to Oliver, October 21, 1864, Botts Letterbook.

[33] Lieutenant Colonel Larkin Smith to James A. Seddon, November 9, 1864, *Official Records,* Ser. I, Vol. III, pp. 800–802.

[34] Coulter, *Confederate States of America, 1861–1865,* p. 180.

IV

The Cotton Bureau

From the beginning of the war, the South had the greatest confidence in the power of King Cotton to procure the necessities for carrying on the conflict. Several departments of the Army and of the civil government eventually had purchasing and impressing agents in the field to assemble huge stores of this valuable exchange medium. In the latter part of 1862 the War Department began to purchase and collect cotton, and "by the fall of 1863 the Ordnance Bureau, Quartermaster, Commissary, Medical Bureau—every important bureau in the War Department—had agents in the field" to gather the cotton for consignment to English firms which were providing extensive military supplies.[1]

In the Trans-Mississippi Department, Major Simeon Hart represented the War Department as a general purchasing agent, while agents of both General Magruder and General Bee competed with Hart for cotton and supplies in Texas. In 1863 General Kirby-Smith established a bureau designed to centralize and coordinate cotton procurement. This chapter will present the story of the use of cotton

[1] Frank L. Owsley, *King Cotton Diplomacy: Foreign Relations of the Confederate States of America,* p. 413. Although the Engineer Bureau did not have a program to buy cotton, it joined the other supply agencies abroad in 1863 when it sent Captain John M. Robinson to England to purchase a long invoice of technical equipment. James L. Nichols, "Confederate Engineer Odd Jobs," *The Military Engineer, LIII* (January–February, 1961), 15.

by the Confederate authorities, particularly in regard to operations affecting the quartermaster, and will attempt to determine the degree of success with which the Cotton Bureau accomplished its mission.[2]

Cotton Control, 1861–1863

Some of the military authorities west of the Mississippi early recognized the possibilities of using cotton in procuring supplies through Mexico.[3] In October, 1861, Brigadier General P. O. Hébert, commanding the Texas Department, instructed his quartermaster to contract with individuals, promising cotton in exchange for arms and ammunition from across the Rio Grande.[4] A year later, War Department effort in Texas began in earnest when Secretary of War Randolph selected for the purpose Major Simeon Hart, a "prominent El Paso citizen" who reportedly was well acquainted with the Rio Grande border. Hart held a quartermaster commission but served as "general purchasing agent" for all government branches.

Shortly after Hart's appointment, another government purchasing agent appeared in the person of Major A. W. McKee, representative of the Treasury Department. An address to the "cotton planters of Texas" appeared in the press on December 27, 1862, announcing that Major McKee, the "General Agent to Purchase Cotton in Louisiana and Texas" wished to buy at least a portion of the cotton crop to procure supplies for the Army.[5] In Arkansas there were, there-

[2] Useful in this connection is Agnes L. Lambie's "Confederate Control of Cotton in the Trans-Mississippi Department" (unpublished M.A. thesis). Some attention to this subject is given in William T. Windham, "The Problem of Supply in the Trans-Mississippi Confederacy," *Journal of Southern History*, XXVII (May, 1961), 158–161.

[3] In his fine history of the King Ranch, Tom Lea calls the mouth of the Rio Grande "the Confederacy's back door." He then develops a case against higher-ranking Confederates for not recognizing the obvious fact that Matamoros was certain to be a "port of world importance, the only Confederate entry for foreign supplies." *The King Ranch*, I, 183, 187.

[4] Hébert to Secretary of War Benjamin, October 24, 1861, *Official Records*, Ser. I, Vol. IV, p. 127.

[5] *Texas Almanac—Extra*, December 27, 1862. McKee's character as a Confederate is blemished by Professor Ludwell H. Johnson's account of an abortive deal between J. H. McKee, cousin of A. W., the Federals, and Major McKee on the eve

fore, now three competing Confederate agencies in the Trans-Mississippi: the War Department (Major Hart); the Treasury (Major McKee and Mr. Block); and the local military-command quartermasters of Generals Hébert and H. P. Bee. In addition, the state of Texas, through its Military Board, had begun to compete with the Confederate agencies.[6]

Of these several agents Major Hart was for some time the most prominent. With offices in San Antonio, Hart organized a group of purchasing assistants, arranged for transportation and forage, and began to contract with various parties for supplies. Planters were advised by local press notices when and where Hart's regional agent could be addressed. A typical notice appeared in the *Galveston Tri-Weekly News* on February 11, 1863: [7]

Having been appointed by Major S. Hart, C. S. A., for the purpose of purchasing cotton, I will visit the planters of Wharton, Brazoria, Matagorda, and Fort Bend Counties. Planters having cotton to sell will please address me by mail at Alleyton.

John Willett
Q. M. Agent

While seeking cotton by such methods, Major Hart proceeded to contract with Nelson Clements, who was to go to Europe to procure rifles, revolvers, shoes, blankets, shirts, hats and incidentals to the extent of a million dollar invoice. For these items Hart promised to pay Clements 100 per cent on the invoice if delivery was made at

---

of the opening of the Red River Campaign: "With the cooperation of his Confederate relative, McKee undertook to prevent the Southerners from burning the cotton when the Northern army began its march up the Red River and then [to] turn it over to Banks when he arrived. In recognition of his valuable services McKee was to receive eighteen cents for every pound he delivered." Probably to make sure that McKee did not hand over the resulting funds to the Confederate Cotton Bureau, payments were to be made to an account in a New Orleans bank, "subject to the joint order of J. H. McKee and Colonel Samuel B. Holabird, chief quartermaster of the Department of the Gulf." Ludwell H. Johnson, *Red River Campaign: Politics and Cotton in the Civil War*, pp. 64–65.

[6] Charles W. Ramsdell, "The Texas State Military Board, 1862–1865," *Southwestern Historical Quarterly*, XXVII (April, 1924), 262.

[7] *Galveston Tri-Weekly News*, February 11, 1863.

Matamoros within the first four months of 1863.[8] Clements, however, made 600 per cent on the contract! A scandal and court-martial of one officer, Major T. S. Moise, assistant quartermaster, resulted from his connection with Clements. Moise was found guilty of allowing a government steamer in his custody, the *General Rusk,* to sail in Clements' service, flying the British flag.[9]

In May the *Sea Queen* arrived at Matamoros from London with a consignment for Hart on the Clements contract. General Bee, commanding at Brownsville, despaired of Hart's efforts to assemble enough cotton to redeem the badly needed cargo, which consisted probably of Enfield rifles. Consequently, Bee asked authority to impress cotton to cover the invoice.[10]

When Hart's agents failed to locate enough cotton to cover his commitments, he, too, urged the War Department to seize all cotton and control all transportation to the Rio Grande. Said Hart, "I see no alternative. It is a question of supply or no supply, and I do not see how the Government can hesitate." [11] Hart's letter excited controversy but no action between Secretaries Seddon and Memminger in Richmond. Memminger, supported by President Davis, held Hart's impressment suggestion to be illegal. Secretary Seddon, angered by the Treasury's delicacy, suggested that Memminger "read" the congressional impressment act and also keep up the value of the currency to prevent the need of resorting to other means to pay for goods.[12]

Although Richmond appeared reluctant to apply drastic meas-

---

[8] Clements to Hart, December 16, 1862, *Official Records,* Ser. IV, Vol. III, p. 566.

[9] Samuel Bernard Thompson, *Confederate Purchasing Operations Abroad,* p. 80. Tom Lea might remind the reader at this point that London commercial circles understood in November and December, 1862, that it was possible to take a cargo of military goods to the Rio Grande and split a 100-per-cent profit with at least one agent there. *The King Ranch,* I, 189–190.

[10] Bee to Magruder, May 22, 1863, *Official Records,* Ser. I, Vol. LIII, pp. 870–871.

[11] Hart to Seddon, May 16, 1863, *ibid.,* pp. 867–868.

[12] Memminger to Davis, June 30, 1863, *ibid.,* pp. 869–870. See Jonnie M. Megee for a study of the application of impressment in the region west of the Mississippi River. "The Confederate Impressment Acts in the Trans-Mississippi States" (unpublished M.A. thesis).

ures, General Kirby-Smith sanctioned Magruder's grant of limited impressment power to Bee. Only the cotton of speculators and contractors was to be affected by the impressment authority.[13] Bee, with his new weapon in reserve, issued a call for cotton and found himself opposed by the LaGrange *Patriot* on the grounds that "a great and fundamental principle of human liberty" was being assailed by such threats of compulsory sale.[14] The *Fort Brown Flag* blamed Hart for failure to fulfill his contracts and suggested that Kirby-Smith "continue his stretch of authority a little further and jayhawk Mr. Hart." [15]

Despite the criticisms, efforts to procure enough cotton to clear Hart's contract continued. In July Hart wrote the War Department that three British ships, the *Sea Queen, Sir William Peel,* and the *Gladiator,* were at the mouth of the Rio Grande "laden with valuable army stores." The cargo of the *Gladiator* consisted of clothing material and almost every type of army stores except munitions. Cotton was to be exchanged at thirty cents a pound for the cargoes, and Hart advised that he had managed to get 12,000 or 13,000 bales.[16] He did not state clearly that he expected to meet his commitments but only that General Magruder's impressment plan was operating to that effect; a month later General Bee wrote Magruder that Major Charles Russell (Bee's quartermaster) had accumulated enough cotton to pay off the *Gladiator* and the *Sea Queen.*[17] Russell's job was made considerably easier by a contract between the Confederate authorities (Magruder and Bee) and the firm of M. Kenedy & Co. The contract, dated April 28, 1863, pledged the services of Messrs. King, Kenedy, and Stillman to the supply of Bee's border troops. In return the government was to deliver 500 bales of cotton per month

---

[13] Yancey to Bee, July 2, 1863, *Official Records,* Ser. I, Vol. LIII, pp. 100–101.

[14] *Patriot* (LaGrange, Texas), July 30, 1863.

[15] Quoted by the *Patriot,* August 6, 1863.

[16] Hart to Seddon, July 13, 1863, *Official Records,* Ser. I, Vol. LIII, pp. 877–878.

[17] Bee to Magruder, August 17, 1863, *ibid.,* p. 892. The often quoted Britisher, Lieutenant Colonel Arthur Fremantle, recorded in April, 1863, that seventy vessels were constantly outside the bar at the mouth of the Rio Grande waiting on two small steamers to ferry cotton to them from Bagdad, the shanty village at the mouth of the river. Lord (ed.), *Fremantle Diary,* p. 6.

for six months to the company. The partners, it is estimated, made about 20 per cent on the deal, or, in specie, about $60,000 each.[18]

Clearly, by the summer of 1863 the cotton situation was so confused with the multiplicity of agents that some system of coordination had to be arranged. The Cotton Bureau was Kirby-Smith's remedy, with a system of purchase hopefully designed to eliminate resorting to the odious impressment device.[19] Close observers of the rising specie value of the royal staple, however, might well have predicted that human nature would require even more rigorous measures than Smith contemplated. Why sell for Confederate paper when the specie was piled up waiting at the Rio Grande, a metallic magnet for lukewarm patriots? [20]

Origins of the Cotton Bureau

By a general order on August 3, 1863, General Smith created a bureau, with Lieutenant Colonel W. A. Broadwell as chief, for the purchase, collection, and disposition of government cotton. When Colonel Broadwell assumed charge, he undertook a survey of the Trans-Mississippi cotton situation as it appeared in the fall of 1863. His report to the Secretary of Treasury in December, 1863, when coupled with a subsequent report to Smith, provides a picture of agents and results at the beginning of 1864: [21]

---

[18] Lea, *The King Ranch,* I, 199–200.

[19] Broadwell to Memminger, December 26, 1863, *Official Records,* Ser. I, Vol. XXVI, Pt. II, pp. 535–539.

[20] The following table illustrates the tremendous rise in the specie value of cotton at Matamoros:

August, 1862	16¢ per lb.
Later in 1862	25¢ " "
April 2, 1863	36¢ " "
November, 1863	80–90¢ " "
1864	82¢ " "
1865	68¢–$1.25 " "

These figures were calculated by Tom Lea from a study of the sources. *The King Ranch,* I, 192, 445 n.

[21] Broadwell to Memminger, December 26, *Official Records,* Ser. I, Vol. XXVI, Pt. II, p. 536; Broadwell to Smith, March 15, 1864, *ibid.,* Vol. LIII, pp. 971–974.

State	Purchased under Direction of	By Whom Purchased	No. of Bales
Arkansas	Treasury	David Block	14,966
Louisiana	J. D. B. DeBow (Treasury)	Dr. C. G. Young, Monroe	5,357
		F. M. Dawson	3,660
	Major A. W. McKee (Treasury)	Lauve & Belknap, Shreveport	28,505
		Francis Webb, Natchitoches	12,556
		Dr. C. G. Young, Monroe	18,926
		T. D. Miller, Washington	1,564
		M. M. Rhorer, Alexandria	9,892
Texas	War Department	Major Simeon Hart	15,997 (estimate)
	Treasury	Henry Sampson	250
			111,673

Of the above 111,673 bales, however, certain dispositions had been made of portions of the total, as follows:

Disposition	No. of Bales	Remarks
Transferred to:		
Lemore & Co.	898	In payment of contract
Capt. J. A. Stevenson	18,028	Stevenson was the Bureau's confidential agent for moving cotton through the enemy lines
Ralli Binachi & Co.	5,357	This transfer supplied the million dollars which Broadwell gave Captains Barrett and Birge
Navy Department	1	On requisition
Engineer Department	1	On requisition

Expended:

Major General Richard Taylor	1,998	Used to fit gunboats
Burned (by troops)	930	Burned in May, 1863, apparently to prevent enemy seizure
Captured by the enemy	50	
Burned (unofficially)	500	
	27,763	

Of the cotton shown in the table, Broadwell preferred not to include Major Hart's purchases. If Hart's figure of 15,997 bales is disregarded, it can be seen that the listed agents had accumulated 95,676 bales by March, 1864.

Among the cotton transfers listed by Colonel Broadwell in the above table was that of 18,028 bales to Captain John A. Stevenson. Stevenson was a New Orleans merchant, an experienced river man with a large knowledge of steamboats, who had first attracted official attention by his plan to construct rams for breaking the blockade.[22] The Confederate ram *Manassas* was of his construction.[23] When the Federals moved up the Mississippi to take New Orleans in the spring of 1862, Stevenson commanded the gunboat *Warrior,* which, along with several other vessels, engaged the United States fleet in an attempt to thwart its plans.[24] In November, 1862, Stevenson approached the War Department with a plan to ship cotton through the New Orleans port. General Benjamin A. Butler, Federal commander, had agreed to an arrangement which was, in effect, legalized blockade running. Stevenson's purposes were regarded with favor by the Confederate Government.[25] In August of 1863, Colonel Broadwell entered into a contract with the Captain which delegated Stevenson as confidential agent for the movement of cotton through

[22] Stevenson to Davis, May 21, 1861, *ibid.,* Ser. IV, Vol. I, pp. 347–348.

[23] Governor T. O. Moore to Benjamin, December 2, 1861, *ibid.,* Ser. I, Vol. VI, p. 773.

[24] Stevenson to Commander J. K. Mitchell, U.S. Navy, April 21, 1862, *ibid.,* pp. 522–525.

[25] Stevenson to Randolph, November 10, 1862 (and endorsement of November 15, 1862), *Official Records,* Ser. I, Vol. XV, pp. 861–863.

the lines.[26] The Lincoln Administration was taken in by Stevenson's proposals, as is explained by Professor Ludwell H. Johnson in his excellent study of Federal interest in cotton in the Trans-Mississippi. Stevenson, a director of the Louisiana State Bank, which was now on the Federal side of the lines, borrowed a large amount of cotton from the Bank. The cotton was well behind the Confederate lines in the Trans-Mississippi. Stevenson proposed to exchange this cotton (which was a frozen asset to the Louisiana State Bank) for a like amount of Confederate-owned cotton on the Ouachita River, which was exposed to Federal capture. The cotton would then be shipped to Europe to the firm of George Arnold Holt and Company of Liverpool, with the Federals permitting the shipment under their belief that they were simply assisting a financial institution loyal to their side. Funds resulting from the sale would then be turned over by the Louisiana State Bank to Stevenson, who would place them at the disposal of Confederate Treasury officials.[27]

Stevenson's story is made more astonishing by the fact that Federal officers captured him on September 6, 1863, at Morgan's Ferry on the Atchafalaya, and reported the affair as follows: "Among the captures yesterday is one John A. Stevenson, of New Orleans, who is an agent of the Confederate Government, buying cotton as basis for their loan. He had considerable Confederate money and drafts, and printed contracts for a large amount of cotton." [28] As this arrest occurred only two weeks after negotiation of his contract with Broadwell, it appears that Stevenson was en route to New Orleans to complete arrangements on that side of the lines.

Stevenson apparently talked his way out of the corner provided by the damning circumstances of his arrest. In mid-January, 1864, he was hard at work with General "Dick" Taylor in moving the cotton through the lines. Of the exposed cotton which had been of major concern to the Confederates, Taylor agreeably reported as

---

[26] Joint statement by Lieutenant Colonel W. A. Broadwell and John A. Stevenson, Shreveport, August 24, 1863, Kirby-Smith Papers.

[27] Johnson, *Red River Campaign*, pp. 68–69.

[28] Major General F. J. Herron to Brigadier General C. P. Stone, September 8, 1863, *Official Records*, Ser. I, Vol. XXVI, Pt. I, pp. 312–313.

follows: "We are now relieved of all Government cotton on the Ouachita, and I consider the arrangement highly satisfactory." [29] It is likely, therefore, that the 18,028 bales reported by Broadwell as transferred to Stevenson got through the lines to accumulate credits in Europe.

The tangled cotton web in Texas evoked a mass of bitter charges and countercharges against and between quartermasters, state officials, planters, and various agents. Kirby-Smith admitted that "the state of the public mind and the tone of public feeling is such that every man jealous of his reputation hesitates about having his name associated with any Government transaction in cotton." [30] Broadwell's unhappy report to Secretary of Treasury Memminger in December, 1863, succinctly summarized the reasons for the deteriorating cotton supply situation:

The policy pursued [in Texas] has been vacillating, and the general management exceedingly bad; a variety of agents and numberless contractors appearing in the market at one time brought the Government in competition with itself, and prices were in consequence rapidly advanced; speculation was rife, and great eagerness manifested to invest the currency in an article by which the money could be converted into a sounder character of funds. Selling cotton for gold, buying up Confederate paper at its depreciation, and reinvesting in our cotton which could be again sent to Mexico, was ascertained to be a profitable business, and led to swindling and bad faith. A system of bogus Government contracts was inaugurated, by which the fortunate few obtained permits giving them freedom from molestation. The cotton was invariably carried out, frequently with the use of conscripts as teamsters, and other assistance from the Government, the contracts rarely ever filled. The bonds that had been given for their faithful performance had no validity in law, and would

[29] Taylor to Kirby-Smith, *Official Records*, Ser. I, Vol. LIII, p. 952.
[30] Parks, *General Edmund Kirby Smith*, p. 294. Proof of this attitude is revealed in a postwar letter of James Calvert Wise, wartime quartermaster general for the state of Louisiana. Writing to Governor J. M. Wells in 1869, Wise emphatically denied ever having had anything to do with cotton during the war. He said he had threatened to resign when Governor H. W. Allen had suggested he administer a cotton purchase program. Allen decided, consequently, to appoint several agents and have them report directly to the Governor. Cotton transactions, therefore, appear not to have been a state quartermaster concern in Louisiana. Wise to Wells, March 28, 1869, James Calvert Wise Papers.

have been forfeited if this were not the case. The public service was embarrassed by a failure to receive what the officers were led to expect, and the necessities of the Government compelled the impressment of the cotton of those who appeared on the Rio Grande without military protection. A species of favoritism was established, which created great dissatisfaction, and continued conflict grew out of the various military orders, which appeared necessary from time to time.[31]

Concurrently with his survey of the cotton situation in the Trans-Mississippi, and his negotiation with Stevenson, Colonel Broadwell began to set up an organization to carry out the work of the Bureau. Two of the first officers assigned to duty with him were Captains N. A. Birge, of Jefferson, Texas (whose operations in other capacities have been discussed previously), and W. W. Barrett, a Nacogdoches merchant in civilian life.[32] Initial orders to these officers directed that they provide transportation to remove government cotton from "exposed localities" to points in the interior where it could be protected from both weather and pillage. Transportation required was to be bought or hired at a reasonable cost. Further, civilians could be hired as teamsters or wagon masters, and soldier details were to be available if required for any purpose. Both transportation and Negroes could be impressed by Birge and Barrett, if necessary. Birge was urged to employ men who were exempt from military service, but if his requirements could not be met this way, the chief of staff, General Boggs, authorized exemptions from military duty to men who would furnish one wagon and team and themselves to work as drivers.[33] The two officers soon assembled a train of 350 wagons with which they moved 7,000 bales from Louisiana to the banks of the Sabine, forty-five miles from Shreveport, where sheds were erected to house the cotton.[34]

Having made provision for transportation and personnel in the fall of 1863, Broadwell was ready to outline his complete plan of

[31] Broadwell to Memminger, December 26, 1863, *Official Records,* Ser. I, Vol. XXVI, Pt. II, pp. 535–538.
[32] Broadwell to Birge, August 23, 1863, Birge Papers, Case 18.
[33] Broadwell to Birge, August 23, 1863, *ibid.*
[34] Broadwell to Memminger, December 26, 1863, *Official Records,* Ser. I, Vol. XXVI, Pt. II, p. 536.

organization to the public in January, 1864. Lieutenant Colonel W. J. Hutchins was to control all the cotton in Texas in the counties south of and including Anderson County. This branch, the Texas Cotton Bureau, was first, for a brief time, under A. W. Terrell, but was taken over by Hutchins in November.[35] Hutchins and his associates, James Sorley, B. A. Shepherd, George Ball, and W. J. Kyle, were assured that their only superior was Kirby-Smith himself and that Smith had promised not to overrule the Texas Bureau without prior conference with its directors.[36] Broadwell urged these gentlemen to strive for honesty and consistency for the sake of public morale. Cotton contracts in Texas made prior to the establishment of the Texas office would continue to be supervised by Broadwell.[37] The remaining portion of Texas was divided into two districts under Birge and Barrett, respectively, who were charged with the purchase of cotton to the extent that planters would sell.[38] In northern Louisiana two agents continued to purchase as they had been, while another agent was assigned to buy cotton in Arkansas for the government account. All three were to report monthly to Broadwell's office in Shreveport.[39] This setup proved to be of brief duration, however, as Broadwell eventually moved to Houston to direct the Texas office personally. In a letter of August 16, 1864, Colonel W. J. Hutchins explained to a correspondent: "I am no longer at the head of the Cotton office. Col. W. A. Broadwell has succeeded me." Hutchins, at this period, signed his letters as "Chief Purchasing Quartermaster." [40]

---

[35] Special Orders No. 198, Headquarters Trans-Mississippi Department, November 22, 1863, *ibid.*, p. 437. See also Captain C. S. West to Broadwell, Shreveport, November 23, 1863, in "Cotton Sold to Confederate States," *Senate Document No. 987*, pp. 310–311. See also Texas Cotton Bureau Letterbook.

[36] Broadwell to Hutchins, *et al.*, November 20, 1863, Texas Cotton Bureau Letterbook. Microfilm copy in writer's possession.

[37] *Ibid.*

[38] Birge's district included Marion, Davis, Bowie, Red River, Cass, Fannin, Grayson, Hunt, Collin, Hopkins, Titus, Cook, Denton, and Upshur counties, while Barrett's district included Harrison, Wood, Kaufman, Dallas, Van Zandt, Henderson, Navarro, Smith, Rusk, Panola, Shelby, Nacogdoches, San Augustine, Sabine, and Cherokee counties. See Circular, Headquarters, Trans-Mississippi Department, January 4, 1864, Birge Papers, portfolio for January 1–May 31, 1864.

[39] *Ibid.*

[40] Hutchins to A. W. Collins, Texas Cotton Bureau Letterbook.

A few days after publication of his original plans, Broadwell obtained a million dollars for the use of Birge and Barrett, and these two officers began their purchases. Broadwell had raised these funds by selling 5,357 bales of cotton which James D. B. DeBow had purchased for the government near the Mississippi River.[41]

Almost at once Broadwell's two officers ran into difficulties with speculators. Barrett wrote Birge that if the Bureau raised its purchase price for cotton to twenty-five cents a pound, the speculators would give thirty cents, and if to thirty cents, the speculators would pay thirty-five cents, etc.[42] Broadwell thought the government should pay twenty-five cents per pound, however, and authorized that price in March, believing that it would please the planters. In regard to speculators, he thought that the matter was "before the patriotism of the people" and that they must "discriminate between those who are working for the Govt, and those of the people who have made large fortunes out of the necessities of the Govt." [43]

In the latter part of 1863, Kirby-Smith had sent Major J. F. Minter, his chief quartermaster, abroad to England to see to contracts already made and to purchase both ordnance and quartermaster stores, with cotton as a basis for payment.[44] But the purchase of cotton was still going so slowly in March, 1864, that Kirby-Smith fretted about meeting the commitments abroad. Broadwell urged Birge and Barrett to start 500 wagons loaded with cotton for San Antonio at the earliest opportunity. The cotton was on hand for this convoy, but the organization of the train was left to the two captains.[45] On March 11 Broadwell ordered the assembly of 2,550 bales "to pay for army stores purchased by Major Minter under the contract with Messrs. Bouldin & Newell for which he ha[d] given

[41] Barrett to Birge, March 4, 1864, Birge Papers, portfolio for January 1–May 31, 1864; Broadwell to Kirby-Smith, March 15, 1864, *Official Records,* Ser. I, Vol. LIII, pp. 971–974.

[42] Barrett to Birge, March 4, 1864, Birge Papers, portfolio for January 1–May 31, 1864.

[43] Captain W. A. Black to Birge, March 4, 1864, Birge Papers, portfolio for January 1–May 31, 1864.

[44] Smith to Davis, November 21, 1863, *Official Records,* Ser. I, Vol. XXII, Pt. II, p. 1074.

[45] Broadwell to Birge, March 5, 1864, Birge Papers, portfolio for January 1–May 31, 1864.

certificates." Colonel Hutchins of the Texas office was to arrange for meeting the demand.

In the meantime, Minter in England was busy making contracts and dispatching shiploads of supplies to the Trans-Mississippi. By the end of 1864 and during the early months of 1865 his shipments had become quite extensive, as is indicated by the following table: [46]

Summary of Invoices of Goods Purchased by Major Minter

Received from	Value of Goods in British Pounds
Major J. B. Ferguson, Q.M. Purchasing agent in England	29,270.19.3
Alexander Ross & Co.	1,944.17.3
Curtis & Harvey	1,149.15.6
Ely Bros.	1,750.13.3
Wiggins Fape & Co.	199.14.6
Alex. Collie & Co.	105. 5.1
Hearon McCulloch & Co.	1,097.16.2
Wm. Middlemore	26.16.3
Helbert & Co.	30.19.6
Major Caleb Huse	217. 3.9
Sinclair Hamilton & Co.	9,805. 8.1
	45,599. 8.7

The purchases listed above were shipped according to the following schedule:

Vessel	From	Date
Ship, *Adelaide*	Liverpool	November 14, 1864
Ship, *Victory*	Liverpool	November 16, 1864
Steamer, *Lark*	Liverpool	December 6, 1864
Ship, *Heinrich Bachman*	Liverpool	December 19, 1864
Ship, *Maria Victoria*	London	November 30, 1864
Ship, *Observador*	London	December 28, 1864
Brig, *Lochalva*	London	January 12, 1865
R. M. Steamer	Southampton	March 2, 1865
R. M. Steamer	Southampton	April 2, 1865

[46] Kirby-Smith Papers. The pound was worth about $4.85 in 1864 (25 to 1 in Confederate treasury notes). Todd, *Confederate Finance,* p. 192.

Typical of invoices signed by Minter was the following:

Date	Items
November 12, 1864	10 bales 50% woolen hose
	(150 doz. per bale)
	41 cases sewed army shoes
	(4,100 prs.)
	31 cases sewed army shoes
	(3,100 prs.)
	98 bales blue-gray blankets
	(75 prs. per bale)
	15 bales blue-gray blankets
	(70 prs. per bale)
	5 bales brown-gray blankets
	(70 prs. per bale)
	2 bales brown-gray blankets
	(75 prs. per bale)
November 29, 1864	5,000 suits, infantry uniform
	5,375 military jackets
	5,350 pairs trousers
December 6, 1864	7 cases stationery
	30 cases army shoes (3,000 prs.)
December 19, 1864	5,000 suits infantry uniform
	150 pairs pantaloons
	117 jackets
	36 cases army shoes (3,600 prs.)
	12 cases sewed Bluchers (1,200 prs.)
	14 bales gray, all-wool shirts (4,884)

All these items were shipped to Havana, intended for the Trans-Mississippi.[47] Apparently, to judge by the stores shipped from

[47] Kirby-Smith Papers. Most European shipments to the Trans-Mississippi arrived via Havana, apparently, although an occasional cargo cleared for Matamoros via St. George's, Bermuda. See Frank E. Vandiver (ed.), *Confederate Blockade Running Through Bermuda 1861–1865: Letters and Cargo Manifests*, pp. 86, 95, 110, 130. For additional accounts of the Lower Rio Grande trade, see Annie Cowling, "The Civil War Trade of the Lower Rio Grande" (unpublished M.A. thesis); and Robert W. Delaney, "Matamoros, Port for Texas during the Civil War," *Southwestern Historical Quarterly*, LVIII (April, 1955), 473–487.

Brownsville, most of Minter's purchases got through to the Rio Grande in late 1864 and early 1865.

Although most of this cargo eventually got through the Rio Grande supply line, the Bureau remained in trouble in trying to meet cotton commitments. Broadwell pressed even harder on Birge and Barrett: government obligations must be met; the general was greatly worried.[48] Reporting to President Davis, Broadwell remarked that his Bureau had no legal foundation and that contractors and speculators were giving a great deal of trouble. Governor Pendleton Murrah of Texas was making a bad situation worse by competing with the Bureau for cotton. By giving permission to planters to ship the same amount of cotton that they sold to the state, Murrah was offering terms which the Confederate authorities could not match. Murrah's intention, wrote Broadwell, was to ship 60,000 bales to Mexico in this manner; such a plan would involve all the baled cotton in Texas.[49] Murrah's competition in May, 1864, had so constrained the Texas Cotton Bureau in meeting commitments for goods in port that Broadwell had directed Birge, at Jefferson, to rush 1,000 wagons of cotton to San Antonio.[50] Difficulties with Murrah were mostly alleviated by July when he and Kirby-Smith decided to agree, but there is evidence that the Texas Military Board continued to export through the winter of 1864.[51]

Perhaps the least of the Bureau's problems, but possibly the most interesting, were holdups of southward bound wagons by armed women who would force wagon masters to kick off several bales of cotton. On October 14, 1864, a "party of armed women" seized four bales from John M. Dollahite in Dallas County, Texas; and on November 7 another distaff force seized two bales from one of Birge's trains passing through Kaufman County. The reader of these notarized accounts may well wonder at the gallant qualities of Con-

---

[48] Broadwell to Birge, March 5, 1864, Birge Papers, portfolio for January 1–May 31, 1864.

[49] Broadwell to Davis, April 6, 1864, *Official Records,* Ser. I, Vol. LIII, pp. 979–980.

[50] Letter of May 5, 1864, Confederate States Army Collection.

[51] Ramsdell, "The Texas State Military Board, 1862–1865," *Southwestern Historical Quarterly,* XXVII (April, 1924), 271.

federate teamsters—but then, these were needy Texas prairie women! [52]

Operations of the Texas Cotton Bureau

The Texas Cotton Bureau in Houston found that one-fourth of its efforts at first were being expended in paying old government debts. By May of 1864 Colonel Hutchins reported the office had procured 6,800 bales at an average cost of $50.00 per bale. Of this $340,000 worth of cotton, one-fourth had been expended to pay claims one or two years old.[53] Large purchases had been made by the office, however, and every branch of service received a variety of items from the cotton sales made by May of 1864. Supplies received included powder, rifles, bayonets, and cannon for the Ordnance Department, and shoes, shirts, calico, cotton goods, leather, stationery, and tools for the quartermaster and commissary stores. Significantly, Hutchins concluded his letter with the remark, "Many large lots of shoes, blankets, and other stores have been offered to me, which I have been unable to procure for want of cotton to pay." [54] Although Hutchins' surviving letterbook in the National Archives contains no grand summary of imported goods, the entries enable one to follow the day-by-day activities of his office. A sampling of this activity probably will serve to illustrate the whole cotton-traffic operation in the last year of the war.

Immediately after their appointment in the fall of 1863, Hutchins and his associates outlined a plan for their assigned area. District lines were drawn and depots named at Alleyton, San Antonio, Hallettsville, Brenham, and LaGrange, with a purchasing officer at each depot. Business agents of "perfectly incorruptible" character were to be located at San Antonio and Eagle Pass to deal "tactfully" with the Mexicans. Actual transportation of the cotton would be left to the quartermaster service, which, Hutchins *et al.* presumed could acquire from conscript sources several hundred noncombatants

---

[52] Birge Papers.
[53] Hutchins to Editor, *Galveston Tri-Weekly News,* May 23, 1864.
[54] *Ibid.*

"shirking military duty" who might be made to work as teamsters.[55] When private parties hauled for the government, the office would pay 10 pounds of cotton from each 100 pounds hauled 100 miles. (Such a toll would have wiped out a shipment from Central Arkansas!) Government rates paid for cotton were set as follows: 8½ cents for "ordinary;" 11½ cents for "good ordinary;" 13 cents for "low middling;" 14½ cents for "middling;" 15½ cents for "good middling." The price of cotton at the Rio Grande at that time varied from about 70 to 90 cents a pound.[56]

From the start, Hutchins refused to give advance exemption from impressment to parties presenting plans for import of commodities needed by the government. The Clements case and others had taught their lesson. The goods had to be already at hand so the invoice, markup and costs could be easily understood by the Bureau. In one case, Captain John E. Garey, acting chief quartermaster for the Trans-Mississippi, wanted to permit J. W. Zacharie to send out 300 bales of cotton on the promise that Zacharie would import grain sacks which he would sell the quartermaster at 75 cents each. Since grain sacks cost over $3.00 in the Confederacy, Garey endorsed the proposal. Hutchins disapproved the plan as contrary to "the policy of this office." Kirby-Smith had promised not to override Hutchins without a conference and here he appears to have lived up to his word, as he made no effort to sustain his chief quartermaster in what might have been regarded as a question of rank.[57]

Hutchins made local contracts with blockade runners who would run greater risks than would the Matamoros importers. Typical was an agreement with Messrs. F. P. Sawyer, F. W. Smith, and J. B. Price in December, 1863, in which these men agreed to "introduce" a large quantity of Enfield, Belgian muskets, quartermaster and medical supplies on "steamers or fast sailing vessels" at Sabine Pass, Galveston, Columbia, the Brazos River, and Port Lavaca. Mer-

---

[55] "Memorandum," noted on Broadwell's letter of November 20, 1863, Texas Cotton Bureau Letterbook.
[56] Hutchins to W. M. Sledge, December 15, 1863, *ibid.;* Hutchins to John Doran, December 18, 1863, *ibid.;* Lea, *The King Ranch*, I, 192.
[57] Hutchins to Garey, December 24, 1863, Texas Cotton Bureau Letterbook.

chandise prices would be settled by a commission, with cotton exchanged at the rate of eight to fifteen cents per pound, according to classification.[58]

Much of Hutchins' time in his first weeks in office went to corresponding with planters who wanted to know procedure. To E. E. Stuart of Marlin, for example, Hutchins explained that his office would pay "specie" prices with "certificates redeemable by Congress" for one-half of the planter's crop which remained after he had paid his tithe and other taxes to the government. The planter would then be allowed to export the other half to the Rio Grande for his personal account.[59]

Hutchins adhered strictly to these basic fifty-fifty principles upon which the Bureau was founded. Consequently, the director found himself daily disapproving one or more propositions involving variations. Often these "deals" bore the tentative or lukewarm endorsement of Confederate officers. All of them purported to be to the advantage of the government if permitted to attain consummation. Recognizing their inability to sift through all these schemes, Hutchins and his associates decided to honor no deviations except for a few efforts by church and charitable associations.[60]

Such rigid regard for regulations probably irritated the speculator and those with patriotic, if peculiarly phrased, purposes.[61] A prime example of Hutchins' caution developed in the case of Messrs. McMerty and Atkisson, who had asked, via Major W. H. Haynes of the Clothing Bureau, to be allowed to export 1,000 bales of cotton to complete a contract for the import of gray cloth. Hutchins disapproved the proposal on the basis of his policy not to endorse a scheme until the goods were already in port. Haynes finally made clear to Hutchins that Kirby-Smith had much earlier acknowledged the contract, that 12,000 to 15,000 yards of cloth were already at Piedras Negras waiting to be redeemed with cotton, and that if Hutchins did not permit passage of the McMerty bales, some

---

[58] Contract of December 7, 1863, *ibid.*
[59] Letter of December 13, 1863, *ibid.*
[60] Daily examples in *ibid.*
[61] Some letters of complaint and appeal appeared each week. *Ibid.*

5,000 winter uniforms would be denied the Army. Hutchins quickly released the cotton with the wry note that he had been supplied much more information on the second set of petition papers than on the first.[62]

Determined efforts of the Waco Manufacturing Company to import cloth-making machinery brought Hutchins over to full endorsement of their enterprise in February, 1864. He already had squelched two or three proposals of prospective manufacturers who wished to export cotton to obtain machinery. These other plans, he believed, if seen through to success, would not produce cloth until after the war; but the determination of the Waco effort finally won his admiration, and he approved their export of 200 bales and promised to buy their product if and when they began production. He then forwarded report of his approval to Department headquarters suggesting full support of the proposed factory.[63]

Railroads and telegraph lines were denied special privileges by Hutchins. He seems to have treated them all alike. When the Star State Telegraph Company applied for a permit to export 200 bales at Eagle Pass to buy supplies for the line, Hutchins rejected the petition with the endorsement that the company charged the government too much for its services anyway.[64]

Another noteworthy contract, designed to supply troops on the Rio Grande, was negotiated by Hutchins on April 30, 1864, with the famous firm of M. Kenedy and Co. (Messrs. Stillman, Kenedy, and King, actually).[65] The contract, which was in effect for the rest

---

[62] Hutchins to Haynes, December 15, 1863, and Haynes to Hutchins, with endorsement, January 1, 1864, *ibid.*

[63] John B. Earle to Hutchins, and endorsement, February 16, 1864, *ibid.*

[64] The Cotton Bureau Letterbook contains several rejections of such scattered requests throughout 1863 and early 1864.

[65] The King Ranch historian, Tom Lea, notes that Richard King and associates were again chosen in 1864, by order of General Magruder, to supply the troops in the Rio Grande theater. Lea (*The King Ranch*, I, 224) understandably follows John Salmon ("Rip") Ford's memoir on the point and decides, finally, that if there was a contract, "it has not been preserved." Reference to the Cotton Bureau Letterbook calls for a slight modification of the story. There was a contract dated April 30, 1864, and the Cotton Bureau, which took no orders from General Magruder, made the arrangements for the supply of Ford's command.

of the war, provided the contractors with cotton or corn at Alleyton, San Antonio, or on the Rio Grande on a cost-plus-19½-per-cent basis. This profit margin was made to look even better by provision that the government would in addition pay for transportation over the river and 2½ per cent more on delivery costs. The contractors promised to charge only "lowest prices practicable." [66]

The Rio Grande military command had ever sought to stay well equipped and, being at the source of supply, their officers should have been able to arrange it somehow. References have been made earlier to efforts in that direction by the quartermaster for General Bee. In May, 1864, Brigadier General J. E. Slaughter asked a permit for Colonel Benavides to export 200 bales in order to pay his troops who had not been paid "in two years." Slaughter warned Hutchins that the men would be driven to join the "smugglers" in order to raise funds. Hutchins approved the proposal without comment. [67]

Increasing transportation trouble caused the Texas Cotton Bureau to arrange in July, 1864, for Major Charles Russell, longtime Rio Grande quartermaster, to head a "Transportation Corps" which would direct the freight traffic between San Antonio and Mexico. Cotton Bureau personnel in Texas were ordered to report to Russell the location and amount of government cotton in their possession so that he could arrange to haul it out. [68]

A typical letter of exemption from Broadwell in July, 1864, involving export of cotton by Messrs. Hall and Chandler, will serve further to illustrate the system operating in the summer of 1864:

The within Cotton is exempted from impressment in transit to San Antonio. Upon its arrival there Capt. T. C. Twichell will receive one half for a/c of the Govt—paying for it 25¢ per lb. in Confederate money and the specie freight 1½¢ on the Govt Half and give the right to export a like quantity—Capt T. will ship the h[a]lf thus acquired by the Gov't. on

[66] Contract in Texas Cotton Bureau Letterbook. Hutchins had earlier applied $23,000 in gold for the supply of Benavides' command on the Rio Grande. *Ibid.*

[67] Letter of May 24, 1864, *ibid.*

[68] Hutchins' circular of July 12, 1864, *ibid.*

Mr. Chandler's trains to the Rio Grande—at the usual rate of freight in Specie.[69]

Even Texas state sovereignty finally gave way to the discipline of the export system. When state officials wished to export 767 bales for certain named exporters, they applied to the Confederate Cotton Bureau for a permit. Endorsing the application with the comment that Governor Murrah and General Kirby-Smith had reached agreement on these matters, Broadwell instructed San Antonio officers to let the cotton through.[70] Broadwell understood that Governor Murrah had become convinced that the Confederate authorities must have at least one-half of the cotton in the state and had agreed to use his influence to get planters to agree to sell to Bureau agents on the fifty-fifty system. Murrah even offered to lend state cotton to help the Bureau meet obligations at the border. General Smith, in turn, agreed to permit some state export, especially a shipment to raise cash to pay interest on state bonds.[71]

Especially irritating to officials of the Cotton Bureau, as it was to all supply officers, was the energy of Trans-Mississippi conscript details in the last year of the war. These zealous people, trying to meet demands for men from every service, apparently remained on the heels of quartermaster teamsters at every turn. Such harassment led the Bureau chief in August, 1864, to refer the matter to Department headquarters, wondering "whether or not the services of the men as soldiers in the field, or as teamsters to supply trains is of more importance to the service at this crisis." [72] Several months later, the acting chief of the Bureau, Captain C. G. Wells, advised Broadwell that the conscript agents had almost brought a stop to cotton

[69] Broadwell to Hall and Chandler, July 23, 1864, *ibid.*

[70] Broadwell to Major A. H. Willie, July 26, 1864, *ibid.* Broadwell, by this date, had moved into personal direction of the Texas Cotton Bureau.

[71] Broadwell to Thomas F. McKinney, July 16, 1864, *ibid.* These state arrangements are possibly the shipments alluded to by Professor Ramsdell in noting evidence of Military Board activity in that connection throughout 1864. "Texas State Military Board, 1862–1865," *Southwestern Historical Quarterly*, XXVII (April, 1924), 272.

[72] Captain C. G. Wells to T. F. McKinney, August 17, 1864, Texas Cotton Bureau Letterbook.

operations. The only remedy, Wells believed, would be rigorous orders from Kirby-Smith providing punishment to conscript personnel who interfered with the trains.[73]

Treasury Direction

Recognizing reluctantly that he must authorize cotton impressment by Bureau quartermasters, Smith published on June 1, 1864, an address appealing to planter patriotism:

These articles can be obtained only by importation. Cotton is the sole means of purchase. In the same lofty spirit of patriotism, which leads your sons and brothers to offer their lives for your protection, will you not sell to the Government the only product, by which their valor can be made effective against the public enemy?

The impressment of Cotton will be avoided if possible. But supplies for the army *must be had*. It is left with you to determine, whether, for the preservation of your homes you will force the Government to resort to impressment.[74]

Smith was well aware that commanders all across the South had, since 1861, been forced on occasion to resort to impressment, especially of horses and wagons. The policy had derived from military necessity and not from any right at law. Complaints of what many Confederates regarded as highhanded tactics, caused Congress in March, 1863, to pass a complex act detailing methods of impressing supplies and setting prices throughout the several theaters of war.[75]

[73] Wells to Broadwell, January 21, 1865, *ibid.* For a study of conscription in the area, see Martha N. Goodlet, "The Enforcement of the Confederate Conscription Acts in the Trans-Mississippi Department" (unpublished M.A. thesis). Frank Vandiver says that the conscript officers were a problem everywhere: "Even some men detailed by the Secretary of War were pressed into conscript camps by over-zealous enrolling officers who were anxious to keep the camps filled so they, themselves, would not have to go to the front. These press gangs were so efficient that the Chief of Ordnance found his department with more machines than he had men to run them in late 1864." Vandiver, *Rebel Brass, The Confederate Command System*, p. 99.

[74] Circular, June 1, 1864, "To the Citizens of the Trans-Mississippi Department," Headquarters, Trans-Mississippi Department, *Senate Document No. 987*, p. 311; General Orders No. 34, June 1, 1864, General Orders of the Trans-Mississippi Department, p. 27.

[75] Coulter, *Confederate States of America*, p. 251.

In the Trans-Mississippi, however, it may be noted, Kirby-Smith was reluctant to approve use of the law.

At least one departmental editor, of the *Washington* (Arkansas) *Telegraph,* heartily supported Smith's call for cotton. "It must be had, or we must succumb. We are gratified to find that, with rare exceptions, the whole community of patriotic cotton growers appreciates this, and cheerfully assents to the order." [76]

The quartermaster was doomed to unpopularity anyway, since he already carried the burden of impressment responsibility. As Professor Coulter has put it, "Youans must be a d—d fool or a quartermaster," became a common expression.

Wild, unfounded charges were spread that one quartermaster officer had made $5,000,000 from his position . . . The quartermasters were in fact generally honest, and this defense of them by Bill Arp was something more than humorous: How consoling to hear the "eloquent remark from a trafficking Shylock, . . . 'I tot I could make some of de monish here 'mong dese officers, but by tam, dese quartermasters too tam hones; I do nothin' wid dem.' " [77]

Despite Kirby-Smith's plea for voluntary sale, public reaction to the Cotton Bureau continued to be bad. Impressment tactics stung the victims into bombarding Richmond with so many complaints that the Bureau was placed under Treasury Department direction. Secretary Seddon probably welcomed an opportunity to transfer the Bureau to Treasury control, a move made mandatory by decisions setting up an intelligent plan for re-establishing the credit of the Confederate States abroad and at home.[78]

Recognizing at last the dire necessity, the Confederate government decided in early 1864 to assume control over foreign commerce. For some time, agents abroad, notably Colin J. McRae and John Slidell, had urged plans for re-establishing Confederate credit in Europe and for centralizing overseas financial direction. As a result, McRae was recognized by the Treasury, War, and Navy

---

[76] Issue of June 22, 1864.
[77] Coulter, *Confederate States of America,* p. 253.
[78] Seddon to Smith, August 3, 1864, *Official Records,* Ser. I, Vol. LIII, p. 1016.

departments as the only agent to dispose of securities in Europe and to apportion funds among the several purchasing agents abroad.[79] Of McRae's effectiveness, Professor Vandiver has suggested: "Had McRae gone to England earlier, blockade-running might have altered the war." [80] On February 6, 1864, Congress approved "A bill to impose regulations upon the foreign commerce of the Confederate States to provide for the public defense." No cotton, tobacco, military and naval stores, sugar, molasses, or rice could be exported unless under conditions laid down by President Davis. Other legislation cut off import of luxury items so as to reserve all shipping space for badly wanted necessities.[81]

Two months later President Davis approved an arrangement by which the Treasury, War, and Navy departments divided responsibility on the marketing of cotton, tobacco, and naval stores. Purchase and transportation would concern the Army; the shipment and sale would concern the Treasury; the construction of the merchant fleet would be a problem for the Navy. Congress appropriated $20 million to purchase additional raw materials to meet government commitments. As Professor Todd has pointed out, "This was the beginning of a centralized plan for the control of cotton at home, corresponding to the reorganization in Europe under McRae." [82]

Although Secretary of War Seddon, because of the new plan, apparently regarded Broadwell as relieved of duty with the Bureau as of August 3, 1864, months passed before Treasury officials in the Trans-Mississippi exercised much control.[83] Colonel Broadwell, whose "qualifications" were "highly appreciated," was directed by Seddon to remain on Kirby-Smith's staff for such duty as Smith

---

[79] McRae's effective efforts are well treated in Charles S. Davis, *Colin J. McRae: Confederate Financial Agent.*

[80] Vandiver, *Rebel Brass,* p. 119.

[81] *Official Records,* Ser. IV, Vol. III, pp. 80–82.

[82] Todd, *Confederate Finance,* p. 192.

[83] Professor Ramsdell, although approving of the regulation act of February 6, 1864, believed that Richmond authorities should not have tried to apply the law in the Trans-Mississippi. The Cotton Bureau was doing as well as could be done by any government agency faced with the realities of the specie frontier at the Rio Grande. Charles W. Ramsdell, *Behind the Lines of the Southern Confederacy,* pp. 118–119.

prescribed, while Hutchins, in Texas, was to serve under Judge P. W. Gray in directing Cotton Bureau operatives.[84] Judge Gray had become in effect Secretary of Treasury of the Trans-Mississippi Department since Congress, on the recommendation of Secretary Christopher G. Memminger, had authorized him "to discharge any duty or function on the other side of the Mississippi which he, the said Secretary, is competent to discharge." [85]

On November 18, 1864, Smith finally ordered the officers concerned to serve under direction of the Treasury, and indications are that they stayed at their posts until the last months of the war.[86] The letterbook of the Texas Cotton Bureau indicates that it was, in effect, Broadwell's journal from July, 1864, to the end of the war. Many letters were signed by Captain C. G. Wells, as "Acting Chief of the Cotton Bureau," but Wells defers to Broadwell throughout.[87] The Galveston Tri-Weekly News, in October, 1864, praised both Broadwell and Hutchins, remarking that Broadwell was a man of "indomitable energy and incessant application to business." [88]

The Treasury prepared to take over the regulation of overland commerce and export to Mexico by publishing orders, which were implemented by General Smith's order of October 3.[89] Since June, 1864, Major Asa H. Willie, as noted in the discussion of Hutchins' activities, had been stationed at San Antonio to issue permits for the export of cotton, tobacco, molasses, rice, military and naval stores. All trains leaving for the Rio Grande had to be cleared through Major Willie's office before departure from either Goliad or San Antonio. By the amended regulations, speculators were further

---

[84] Seddon to Smith, August 3, 1864, Official Records, Ser. I, Vol. LIII, p. 1016.

[85] Todd, Confederate Finance, pp. 23–24.

[86] General Orders No. 88, General Orders, Trans-Mississippi Department, p. 67. Near the end of the war, on February 15, 1865, the Treasury Department recommended the appointment of Thomas F. McKinney of Austin, Texas, to head the office of chief of the Cotton Bureau of the Trans-Mississippi Department. Todd, Confederate Finance, pp. 23–24.

[87] The last entry in the Letterbook, a minor dispatch regarding rope and bagging, is dated May 17, 1865.

[88] Galveston Tri-Weekly News, October 7, 1864.

[89] Amended Regulations, Implementing Act of February 6, 1864, approved by President Davis, August 3, 1864, General Orders No. 77, October 3, 1864, General Orders, Trans-Mississippi Department, pp. 68–73.

stifled and the government benefited in that one-half of all exports continued to be on government account.[90] Under this system, as under Hutchins' older orders, when a planter agreed to sell an amount of cotton to the quartermaster at government prices, he was issued a permit to export a like amount through Willie's channels to the Rio Grande. Such permits had to be recorded in Shreveport by Captain W. A. Black. Ultimately, customs officers at the border picked up the permit, cancelled it, and returned it to Black at Trans-Mississippi headquarters.[91]

None of this Treasury system appears to be so significantly different from the established procedures of the Cotton Bureau as to justify a conclusion that there was any improvement in efficiency in the Trans-Mississippi. The new regulations of 1864 certainly gave stimulus to Confederate status abroad. European enthusiasm for Confederate bonds and contracts was somewhat restored. With firm government control at hand at last, cotton credits began to build up.[92] In the Trans-Mississippi Department, however, the personnel administering the system did not change. Improvement there came simply from absolute military control of a situation which had to be strictly policed.

Summary and Conclusions

Total quantities of supplies procured by the Cotton Bureau during its period of operations cannot be determined, because of diverse and overlapping sources of information.[93] Shipments from Major J. F. Minter to the Trans-Mississippi (November, 1864, to April, 1865) have already been recorded here. Probably most of these items reached their destination. Sources also contain a report of Lieutenant Colonel Hutchins for the work of his office up to May,

[90] General Orders No. 35, June 4, 1864, and General Orders No. 77, October 3, 1864, in *General Orders, Trans-Mississippi Department,* pp. 27, 70.
[91] Examples with endorsements are in the Birge Papers, Case 11.
[92] Todd, *Confederate Finance,* pp. 193–194.
[93] An attempt was made by William Diamond to summarize the total imports of the Confederacy, but he concluded that the "diverse quantity of those importations cannot be determined." However, he said, they formed "almost the entire source of supply for the Trans-Mississippi Confederacy." William Diamond, "Imports of the Confederate Government from Europe and Mexico," *Journal of Southern History,* VI (November, 1940), 502.

1864, some of which was local purchase and some of which was blockade running; but probably most of the items were imports from Mexico. And there is Colonel Hutchins' report, which was printed in the *Houston Tri-Weekly Telegraph* under the title, "The Head of the Late Cotton Bureau." The report, a summary of the purchases made by his office, is the best piece of available evidence for the magnitude of procurement in the Trans-Mississippi through the medium of cotton. Hutchins' report revealed that the Texas office had handled to the end of 1864, 32,000 bales,[94] which had been used to purchase the following:[95]

5,000	reams	paper and stationery
$100,000	worth of	medicines
15,000	" "	commissary stores
1,300,000	" "	ordnance
30,000	" "	saddler's and shoemaker's stores
2,400 prs.		pants
32,650	shorts	
230,000 yds.		cotton goods (mixed)
77,000 "		satinet
67,000 "		army cloth
25,000 "		flannel
22,000 prs.		socks
18,600 "		blankets
18,000 yds.		mosquito net
64,000 prs.		shoes and boots
200,000 yds.		bagging
245,000 lbs.		bale rope
2,400 pieces		Mexican bagging

[94] Apparently the best source for a final record of the amount of cotton handled by the Texas Cotton Bureau is "Statement B (Texas): List of persons who sold cotton to the Confederate States through the Texas Cotton Bureau, located at Houston, Texas, and operated under direction of the Confederate Military Department of the Trans-Mississippi," *Senate Document No. 987*, pp. 261–307. This tabulation, compiled from incomplete records of the Texas Cotton Bureau, indicates that 49,330 bales were purchased by the Bureau, but much of the cotton was not paid for or delivered. The statement includes transactions from April, 1863, to February, 1865, indicating that some of the earlier purchases were made by Treasury agents before the Bureau was organized.

[95] Cited by Lambie, "Confederate Control of Cotton in the Trans-Mississippi Department" (unpublished M.A. thesis), pp. 87–88.

The volume of goods appeared to be accelerating at the end of 1864. Captain F. J. Lynch, quartermaster at Brownsville, reported the following mass of goods shipped via his office to San Antonio and Alleyton in the last three months of the year: [96]

                600,000 lbs. army stores
                 19,700 prs. shoes
                 14,000 prs. blankets
                 14,000 yds. gray army cloth
                  8,000 yds. gray satinet
                 80,000 yds. brown army drilling
                 50,000 yds. sheeting
                 12,000 yds. duck
                 20,000 woolen shirts
                 18,000 drawers
                 20,000 yds. flannel
                 50,000 lbs. leather
                 10,543 lbs. sheet iron for mess kettles
                 72,000 lbs. bar iron
                100,000 lbs. chains, axes, hardware
                      4 cases lint
                      8 cases thread
                      2 cases needles, thimbles
                    200 oz. quinine
                    200 lbs. blue mass
                    100 oz. morphine and other medicines
                     50 cases stationery
                 12,000 reams paper
              2,000,000 caps

Captain Lynch reported goods arriving in such quantity that he could predict a six months' supply for the Trans-Mississippi would be available by March 1865.[97]

These reports and the other evidence presented in the foregoing account, despite their diversity, permit the conclusion that the Trans-Mississippi Department had geared itself to depend heavily on

[96] "What Becomes of the Cotton," *Washington Telegraph,* January 4, 1865.
[97] *Ibid.*

trade through Mexico for the supplies necessary to carry on the war. Local stocks of merchants were exhausted in the first months of the war, and after the Department was cut off from the east the military looked to cotton as a means of survival. The War Department early took steps to export this item through a special agent, but, as that officer failed, Kirby-Smith expanded his increasingly bureaucratic system to include a special bureau for the handling of cotton. Speculation by private individuals was an early problem confronting the Cotton Bureau. Another problem was the competition of the state of Texas, which hindered the Bureau for some months until Governor Murrah agreed to cooperate. Not the least of vexations for Bureau officials, especially in the last months of the war, was the constant interference with Bureau teamsters and personnel by conscript agents. This problem, due to its nature, was probably never resolved. Always a major problem was the steady depreciation of Confederate currency and bonds, making purchases by Bureau agents extremely difficult.

The Confederate government finally recognized, by the spring of 1864, that it must demand full control of blockade running and international trade. By an act of February 6, 1864, private export was forbidden. Firm government control of cotton export and resulting imports served to raise Confederate credit abroad considerably. The loss of such ports as Mobile, Wilmington, and Charleston in early 1865, however, destroyed serious hope for a supply plan anywhere except in the Trans-Mississippi, where blockade running and Matamoros trade continued to gain in strength right up to the end of the war.[98]

[98] A recent student of the blockade on the Texas coast notes that the blockading squadron in the area was increased 300 per cent in 1865 (from seven to twenty ships). "Even after such precautions only the final fall of the South ended blockade running into Texas ports." Alwyn Barr, "Texas Coastal Defense, 1861–1865," *Southwestern Historical Quarterly*, XLV (July, 1961), 30–31. Evidence of the volume of trade at the mouth of the Rio Grande is cited by Lea most emphatically when he states that the number of ships seen at Bagdad had risen to 200 or 300 in early 1865. Lea, *The King Ranch*, I, 192.

V

Transportation: Supply and Maintenance

The supply of transportation equipment in the first two years of the war involved all Confederate quartermaster officers. Post quartermasters, especially, operated wagon and harness shops and purchased horses, mules, and oxen for the service. The control of the railroads early came under quartermaster direction, and in the east, the quartermaster general placed Major W. S. Ashe, former president of the Wilmington and Weldon, in the position of superintendent of all transportation of troops and military stores via railroads.[1] As the war broadened in scope, a special staff section in the Richmond Quartermaster Bureau began to supervise supply and maintenance of all field transportation in the Confederacy.[2] In accord with this policy, General Kirby-Smith, in January, 1864, set up a bureau for like purposes in the Trans-Mississippi.[3]

This chapter will treat of transport problems in the Trans-Mississippi from 1861 to 1864, examine the operations of the Field Transportation Bureau, and survey briefly the wartime railroad situation in the Department.

[1] Charles W. Ramsdell, "The Confederate Government and the Railroads," *American Historical Review*, XXII (July, 1917), 799.
[2] General Order No. 76, Adjutant and Inspector General's Office, Richmond, October 17, 1862, *Official Records*, Ser. IV, Vol. II, p. 126.
[3] General Order No. 3, January 13, 1864, *General Orders, Trans-Mississippi Department*, p. 2.

Transportation Problems, 1861–1864

In the first year of the war individual unit quartermasters, or state officers before transfer of their troops to Confederate service, purchased or otherwise acquired teams and wagons for organizational transportation. In Missouri, in August, 1861, Brigadier General Jeff Thompson, commanding the Missouri State Guards, directed the purchase of equipment for an "artillery, ammunition and cannon train." [4] At New Madrid, Missouri, Brigadier General G. J. Pillow, "seized" approximately 100 wagons in that locale. Another 103 wagons had been sent from sources at Memphis. Pillow reported that he would require yet another 100 wagons to move his force without resorting to shuttle methods. [5]

Appeals to the people appeared in Arkansas and Texas newspapers asking those who could to "spare their teams, to come to the rescue of the Government." For example, the Confederate quartermaster at Dallas advertised in December, 1862, for any wagons the citizenry could offer to haul supplies between San Antonio and Austin. [6]

In the meantime Texas state officials equipped some troops with transport equipment. The "Deputy-Quartermaster and Commissary-General" advised Confederate Quartermaster Major Sackfield Maclin in November, 1861, that 145 mules, 8 horses, and 41 wagons with harness had been provided Colonel W. H. Parsons' regiment of volunteer cavalry. The mules cost the state $141.55 each, the horses $125 each; wagon and harness cost $172.60 a set. The equipment transported the regiment to Hempstead. [7] The incident illustrates the efforts of the state of Texas.

---

[4] Thompson to General R. V. Richardson, New Madrid, Missouri, August 6, 1861, *Official Records,* Ser. I, Vol. III, p. 632.

[5] Pillow to Polk, August 21, 1861, *ibid.,* p. 668.

[6] Appeal by Captain Thomas Rector, A. Q. M., November 6, 1861, *Daily State Journal* (Little Rock, Arkansas), November 6, 1861; advertisement in *Dallas Herald,* December 13, 1862.

[7] J. C. Kirbey to Major Maclin, acting chief quartermaster, Texas, C.S.A., November 11, 1861, portfolio, "Miscellaneous letters concerning Civil War 1861–1865," in Miscellaneous Records of the Quartermaster and Commissary Departments.

In Louisiana initial sources were soon exhausted; consequently, Major General Richard Taylor, upon assuming command in the area in the summer of 1862, found that his command lacked iron, harness, leather, and teams, which he promptly requisitioned from the Texas District.[8]

Congressional investigation of the various staff sections of the War Department in the winter of 1861 resulted in a summary report on the efficiency of the Quartermaster's Department. In regard to transportation, the investigating committee remarked that Confederate supply was inadequate and would continue to be inadequate even if transportation authorized by Army regulations was somehow arranged for each troop organization.[9]

In the fall of 1862 the central office of the inspector of field transportation was established in Richmond. Major W. L. Cabell, at the time chief quartermaster of the Trans-Mississippi Department, responded to orders from that office with a report of transport equipment in his province.[10] Two months later, in March, 1863, the Richmond office specified personnel arrangements for organizational wagon trains. Each regimental or battalion quartermaster should have one wagon master and one clerk detailed from the command. Brigade and divisional quartermasters could call for the same assignments if they were required. Commissary, ordnance, and quartermaster trains might have a detailed or hired wagon master for each ten teams, at a maximum wage of $50.00 per month. A superintending wagon master, at a salary of $75.00, was authorized for trains having as many as fifty teams.[11]

In May of 1863, a War Department general order laid down several instructions for the guidance of all officers handling field transportation. Artillery horses were badly needed, and all post and depot quartermasters were ordered to collect suitable horses and to

---

[8] Taylor to Hébert, October 19, 1862, *Official Records,* Ser. I, Vol. XV, p. 838.

[9] Committee report to Congress, January 29, 1862, *ibid.,* Ser. IV, Vol. I, p. 885.

[10] Circular, January 31, 1863; *Arkansas Patriot,* February 12, 1863.

[11] Circular, Quartermaster General, Richmond, March 24, 1863, *Official Records,* Ser. IV, Vol. II, p. 455.

report accessions to Major A. H. Cole for disposition.[12] More instructions in October, 1863, charged Cole with control of all transportation equipment in the Confederate States. Field armies could, however, in emergency, perform any of the functions of the transportation branch, if no regularly designated officer of Major Cole's department was available to them. Further, the Richmond Quartermaster Bureau divided the Confederacy into districts, assigning to each of them an inspector of the Field Transportation Bureau. Chief quartermasters of field armies would make their requisitions for transportation to the chief inspector in their district.[13]

The Field Transportation Bureau

In keeping with this policy, on December 30, 1863, Captain F. Ducayet assumed the mantle of "inspector of field transportation" within the Trans-Mississippi.[14] As artillery units lacked horses, Ducayet directed depot and other quartermasters involved in general procurement to transfer horses unfit for field service to civilians in part payment for good artillery horses. The obvious difference in value, as ascertained by disinterested parties, was paid the civilian as additional compensation.[15]

Handling of livestock in routine transportation duties resulted in the loss or death of a certain percentage of the animals. The precise accounting system prescribed for the care of public property required notarized affidavits from the responsible quartermaster on such occasions, and the extant records of such officers contain many examples of these statements. Local county notaries usually took the oaths of wagon masters or persons immediately responsible, and the official paper was then filed by the quartermaster as a credit voucher.[16]

[12] General Orders No. 60, Adjutant and Inspector General, Richmond, May 13, 1863, *ibid.*, p. 552.
[13] General Orders No. 142, Adjutant and Inspector General, Richmond, October 30, 1863, *ibid.*, p. 914.
[14] General Orders No. 60, December 30, 1863, *General Orders, Trans-Mississippi Department*, p. 38.
[15] Circular, Headquarters, Trans-Mississippi Department, January 11, 1864; *Galveston Tri-Weekly News*, January 12, 1864.
[16] Examples are found in Birge Papers, portfolio for January 1–May 31, 1864.

A quick turnover of leadership in the office of the Trans-Mississippi chief inspector brought first Major J. Horace Lacey and then Major C. D. Hill into the position of responsibility. Working under Major Hill was Captain (later Major) Ed A. Burk, "Chief of Field Transportation in Texas," with offices in Houston. In March, General Magruder ordered that no impressment of field transportation be made without Captain Burk's approval.[17] The Field Transportation Bureau, by February, 1864, operated shops in Texas producing 196 wagons, 900 sets of harness, and 360 saddles per month. Burk placed heavy requisitions for hoop iron and other supplies with Hutchins' Texas Cotton Bureau.[18]

The supply of horses remained a constant concern of Hill's people throughout the remainder of the war. In March, 1864, orders were issued in the Trans-Mississippi providing that a board of survey in each of the military districts be responsible for the reclassification of all worn-out cavalry horses. Such animals, derived from this source, could be used by the artillery if in good condition. Those not suited for the artillery were tagged for general hauling. Privately owned horses (those owned by cavalrymen) placed in class 1 were purchased by the quartermaster for $250 each. Class 2 horses brought $150 each. Regular pools of horses were thus created, out of which the Transportation Bureau attempted to fill subsequent requisitions.[19]

The baggage train of the enemy several times furnished a source of supply for Kirby-Smith's transportation offices. Such a system of procurement sometimes worked in reverse, but several Confederate after-action reports give evidence of replenishment at Federal expense.

At the end of March, 1864, when Federal Major General N. P.

[17] General Orders No. 71, Headquarters, District of Texas, New Mexico and Arizona, March 18, 1864, as printed in *Galveston Tri-Weekly News*, March 30, 1864.

[18] E. A. Burk to Hutchins, July 15, 1864, Texas Cotton Bureau Letterbook; Felgar, "Texas in the War for Southern Independence" (unpublished Ph.D. dissertation), p. 416.

[19] Special Orders No. 76, March 29, 1864, Headquarters, Trans-Mississippi Department, as printed in *Galveston Tri-Weekly News*, April 8, 1864.

Banks launched his Red River Campaign against Shreveport and the cotton resources of East Texas, Kirby-Smith's quartermasters collected all the wagons below Mansfield and Pleasant Hill, Louisiana, to make up a wagon train for Taylor's successful forces of defense.[20] Taylor was soon to augment this train considerably by relieving Banks of most of his—over 200 wagons and about 1,000 mules. In Arkansas, in the campaign paralleling Banks' effort, Federal retreat yielded the Confederacy 800 wagons and 4,000 mules.[21] General J. F. Fagan's action at Mark's Mills, Arkansas, on April 24 netted a capture of 112 wagons and 676 mules with harness, while much equipment was perforce burned on the field. Following the action, the inspector of field transportation in Arkansas went to the site and salvaged iron from the burned wagons.[22] Despite these gains, Major Hill told headquarters in June that an "immense quantity of transportation" was still required. Many of the captured wagons were in bad shape, he reported, but were being refitted in shops at Camden, Arkansas.

Major Hill had held off taking over all supply responsibility in the Department until organizational details, shops, and personnel got into operation. By June 29, 1864, he was ready with an announcement of plans. He had divided the Trans-Mississippi into four subdistricts, with a major in charge of each.[23] His organization for Texas placed officers and shops at Dallas, Tyler, Rusk, Mt. Pleasant, Paris, Waco, and Hempstead, with Major Burk supervising all operations in the state. Through newspaper notices, Burk called for the hire of civilian wheelwrights, blacksmiths, carpenters, saddlers, and harness makers. Such skilled artisans and mechanics could

[20] Smith to Taylor, March 31, 1864, *Official Records,* Ser. I, Vol. XXXIV, Pt. I, p. 516; Taylor to Boggs, June 23 and June 24, 1863, *ibid.,* Vol. XXVI, Pt. I, pp. 210–211. Other stores captured included 5,000 new Enfield and Burnside rifles, several 30-pound Parrott guns, and $2 million worth of commissary and quartermaster stores. Hill's endorsement, May 7, 1864, *ibid.,* Vol. XXIV, Pt. III, p. 802.

[21] *Ibid.*

[22] Morgan to Hill, May 2, 1864, *ibid.,* pp. 801–802.

[23] Hill to Cole, June 5, 1864, *ibid.,* Ser. I, Vol. XXXIV, Pt. IV, p. 645. Full responsibility was placed on Hill by General Orders No. 45, June 15, 1864, *General Orders, Trans-Mississippi Department,* p. 40. Hill to Cole, August 10, 1864, *Official Records,* Ser. I, Vol. XLI, p. 1052.

apply for employment at any of the transportation shops in those towns named.[24]

By November, 1864, Hill had extended his program to include additional shops at Washington and Camden, Arkansas, and at Shreveport, Keatchie, and Alexandria, Louisiana. Results were detailed in a report entitled "Army's means of transportation in the Trans-Mississippi Department." The report may be summarized as follows: [25]

Districts	Horses	Mules	Oxen	Wagons	Ambulances
Louisiana	962	6,170	90	1,176	114
Arkansas	581	7,204	347	1,526	96
Texas	190	1,344	466	485	39
Indian Territory	45	1,477	682	356	31
	1,778	16,195	1,585	3,543	280

Hill's report reflected optimism as he listed an abundance of transportation for armies in the field, distributed, as indicated, in accordance with a general order for May 6, 1864: [26]

1 six-mule wagon to each 100 men
1 " " " " " regimental headquarters
1 " " " " " medical staff
1 " " " " " brigade headquarters
2 " " wagons " " divisional headquarters
3 " " " " " corps commander
4 " " " " " division for field hospital service
1 " " wagon " " battery of 100 men
2 " " wagons " " field battery

The *Houston Tri-Weekly Telegraph* commented approvingly upon the efforts of Hill and Burk, declaring that some of the "most important and useful establishments which have been put in opera-

---

[24] Advertisement in *Galveston Tri-Weekly News,* September 7, 1864.

[25] Hill to Cole, November 15, 1864, *Official Records,* Ser. I, Vol. XLI, Pt. IV, p. 1049.

[26] Hill to Cole, August 10, 1864, *ibid.,* p. 1053; General Orders No. 19, *General Orders, Trans-Mississippi Department* (1864 series), p. 11.

tion since the beginning of the war, and to which our people can point with pride, are the workshops of the field Transportation Department in this state." [27]

While Trans-Mississippi resources slowly improved in 1864, at least until the fall, Virginia theater wants increased, and Lieutenant Colonel Cole from Richmond, as early as May, began to call on Kirby-Smith for horses. Smith failed to comply, as captured and purchased animals were being absorbed into his own units. In August, 1864, Cole asked the War Department to send an officer to Mexico to purchase animals, but no action had been taken by February 1, 1865. On that date Cole told his superiors that he was still calling on the Trans-Mississippi for animals but feared that several months must pass before any aid could be expected from Kirby-Smith. If the government would grant 350,000 pounds sterling or gold, he said, 15,000 animals could be procured in Mexico and Texas at $60.00 per head.[28]

In the Trans-Mississippi, lack of funds had from the first restrained Major Hill's activities. In a Richmond communication of November 15, 1864, Hill emphasized his predicament, common to Confederate supply personnel everywhere: "Nothing will strengthen my efforts or the efforts of my officers more than prompt payments for property purchased." [29] In the face of such credit difficulties, Hill's comparative successes were worthy of commendation.

Railroad Transportation

The importance of the Southern railroads in transporting supplies and men to the armies in the field was obvious from the outset to the military command. In the summer of 1861, W. S. Ashe, former president of the Wilmington & Weldon Railroad, was commissioned major and assistant quartermaster in order to superintend the movement of military freight and personnel on "all the Railroads, North and South, in the Confederate States." As it turned out, Major Ashe

[27] As reported in *Dallas Herald,* February 23, 1865.

[28] Cole to Lawton, February 1, 1865, *Official Records,* Ser. IV, Vol. III, pp. 1087–1089.

[29] Hill to Cole, November 15, 1864, *ibid.,* Ser. I, Vol. XLI, Pt. IV, p. 1049.

apparently became little more than a traveling inspector in that first year, for Quartermaster General Myers chose to keep rail affairs close to his own fingertips.

In December, 1862, rail transportation was taken from the control of the quartermaster, and a special War Department official, Colonel William M. Wadley, began to direct the traffic, negotiate with the railroads, and issue regulations. Myers objected strongly, reminding the War Department that although his office was responsible for all transportation, Wadley was not even under his jurisdiction. The Confederate Senate having failed to confirm Wadley's appointment in May, 1863, Captain F. W. Sims took over his duties, and in August, 1863, the railroads came back under control of the Quartermaster's Department.[30]

In the Trans-Mississippi the railroads never played the major part that they did in the east, but their contribution was nevertheless significant. The Vicksburg and Shreveport (western terminus actually Monroe, not Shreveport), in particular, was instrumental in the transportation of supplies across the Mississippi from 1861 to 1863. In Texas there were ten railroads, boasting in 1861 a total of 468 miles. The small network extending from the Louisiana border through Houston to the southwestern interior was by far the most important, as it tapped the rich cotton and sugar land of that area. The Texas and New Orleans, which ran to the Sabine River at Orange, Texas, moved thousands of men to Louisiana in the early years of the war, while the Galveston, Houston and Henderson was of great service to General Magruder in the recapture of Galveston.[31] In northeast Texas a short piece of track connected Marshall with Shreveport. From Houston, three fingers projected north, south, and west to railheads at Brenham, Millican, Alleyton, and Columbia.[32] Each of these railheads naturally became an important quartermaster installation or depot.

[30] Ramsdell, "The Confederate Government and the Railroads," *American Historical Review*, XXII (July, 1917), 794–810.

[31] S. G. Reed, *A History of the Texas Railroads and of Transportation Conditions Under Spain and Mexico and the Republic and the State*, p. 126.

[32] See map opposite page 34 in Charles S. Potts, *Railroad Transportation in Texas*, Bulletin No. 119, The University of Texas.

All these lines came under the jurisdiction of the military and were put to all possible use, but as they were undeveloped and limited in extent, their contribution was perforce minor as compared to that of wagon and water transportation. The several little lines on the eve of the outbreak of war were apparently about to make connections to the northwest and the south. Had the war been delayed a few years until such connections had been made, Texas would undoubtedly have played a much larger role in the conflict than it did.[33]

[33] John Edwin Bramlette, "Railroad Development in Texas before 1861" (unpublished M.A. thesis), p. 101.

VI

Payrolls, Claims, and Money Troubles

An important duty of the Quartermaster's Department was that of paying, or attempting to pay, military personnel such wages as were prescribed by *Regulations*. In addition to the payroll, almost every other general expense of the Army was turned over to these officers for settlement.[1] Various illustrations of these other functions, and malfunctions for want of funds, have been given in earlier pages. Attention will now be concentrated on the operations of the Pay Bureau in the Trans-Mississippi Department, and some account given of quartermaster action in trying to meet these obvious fiscal obligations along with those growing out of civilian claims against the Army.

Prescribed Duties of the Paymasters

The 1861 edition of the Confederate *Army Regulations* was merely a hurried adaptation of the 1857 edition of United States *Army Regulations,* and details of procedure were frequently omitted. In 1862, however, the duties of the quartermaster in regard to payroll functions were fully set down. The quartermaster general was required to make "timely" remittance to the quartermasters and commanding officers of the several pay districts, and pay arrears for

[1] *Army Regulations Adopted for the Use of the Army of the Confederate States,* pp. 120–121.

periods longer than two months were to be especially avoided.[2] How ironical such rigid doctrine must have seemed to all concerned in the difficult years that followed!

Payments, except to officers and discharged soldiers, were made on muster lists and payrolls which were signed by the commanding officer of the company or detachment. Officers were paid on certified accounts and discharged soldiers on a separate form or certificate. Pay stoppages were entered on the payrolls whenever necessary to reimburse the government for the loss of arms, equipment, or public property, or to pay fines for courtmartial sentences. After each payment, four reports were rendered the quartermaster general: (1) an estimate of funds required for succeeding months; (2) an abstract of payments (with vouchers); (3) a general account current in duplicate; and (4) a monthly statement of funds and disbursements. Separate accounts and vouchers were kept for the regular Army and for volunteers and militia.[3] These several provisions remained in force throughout the war.

Claims

An additional concern of the quartermaster was that of the settlement of claims for supplies consumed by troops. Special quartermaster claims officers were detailed after October, 1862, to examine witnesses, assemble testimony, and pay valid claims. When claims were adversely reported, the claims officer forwarded the proceedings of his investigation to the quartermaster general for possible settlement by the Congress. Typical claims considered were those involving consumption of growing crops, injuries to fences, or damage to buildings rented or impressed by quartermasters.[4]

Previous to these regulations no standard procedure had been followed. Major J. F. Minter, when quartermaster at San Antonio, paid claims presented to him in October, 1862, provided they were

[2] Ibid.
[3] Regulations of the Army of the Confederate States, 1862, Containing a Complete Set of Forms, pp. 81–82.
[4] Regulations of the Confederate States for the Quartermaster's Department, Including the Pay Branch Thereof, pp. 174–175.

duly certified by other Confederate quartermaster officers and authenticated by a magistrate.[5] The quartermaster general at Richmond received all sorts of requests for indemnity from claimants scattered across the Confederacy.[6]

In March, 1864, Captain John C. Ransom, following the regular procedure for settling clams for supplies consumed, published a notice in the Galveston paper that he would hear claims at several plantations near Camps Wharton, Velasco, and Sidney Johnston. Troops stationed at these places had consumed a quantity of supplies, for which settlement had not yet been made.[7] A week later Captain Udolpho Wolfe, assistant quartermaster in the district, announced arrangements for his two agents at Richmond and Wharton, Texas, respectively, to pay old accounts for horses, mules, wagons, etc., taken by the Army.[8] Both these notices are illustrative of the manner in which such matters were handled.

Two months later, in June of 1864, Congress provided for a claims officer in each congressional district to investigate all claims, under the direction of the nearest post quartermaster, in regard to forage, provisions, sheep, cattle, hogs, horses, mules, teams, and wagons which had either been furnished the Army by the owner or informally impressed without remuneration to the owner.[9]

The Pre-Smith Period in the Trans-Mississippi

Because the burdens of the Confederate Quartermaster's Department were obviously to be formidable, proposals were made early in the war to divorce the Pay Bureau from the jurisdiction of the Department. In April, 1861, Secretary of War L. P. Walker recommended the separation of these two agencies—something the United States Army had already accomplished. If this was not done, Walker said, a greatly augmented Quartermaster's Department would be

[5] Galveston Tri-Weekly News, October 1, 1862.
[6] For example, Myers to H. V. Jones, September 20, 1862, Birge Papers, Case 12.
[7] Galveston Tri-Weekly News, March 30, 1864.
[8] Ibid., April 8, 1864.
[9] Act of June 14, 1864. See Lester and Bromwell, Digest of the Military and Naval Laws, pp. 309–310.

required. He urged a separate Pay Bureau.[10] In January, 1862, the special congressional committee investigating the several staff departments made the same recommendation. A separate pay department was needed, the committee said, with regular "paymasters" as in the Federal Army; the regimental quartermasters, however, under the proposed plan, would still draw funds and make payments to their own troops.[11] Nothing came of these recommendations for separate jurisdictions, and the payroll responsibility remained in the Quartermaster's Department. The *Regulations* now grouped these duties under "Pay Bureau of the Quartermaster's Department."

The records of Captain N. A. Birge, which have been so often cited on other pages in this paper, indicate that he was able to meet his payroll quite regularly while on duty with Major R. P. Crump's Battalion of Texas Cavalry in 1861 and 1862.[12] On April 16, 1862, at Devall's Bluff, Arkansas, he handed over $20,000 in paymaster and quartermaster funds to the acting quartermaster of the 1st Cavalry Brigade.[13] His troops, at least, and probably others of the Trans-Mississippi, were regularly paid in the early part of the war.

A recent student of the pay and morale problem in the Trans-Mississippi, Harry N. Scheiber, notes, however, that General Theophilus Holmes found the Department months in arrears when he assumed command in August, 1862.[14] Holmes, in his initial report to the War Department, painted a somber picture of conditions in that theater. Obligations to civilians for supplies totalled $13 million.[15] The War Department had already decided that something had gone wrong in the disbursement system of General Earl Van Dorn, Holmes' predecessor, and blame hovered around the head of Captain John D. Adams, paymaster in the area. Richmond figures showed the Arkansas District to have received $33 million in Confederate currency since Van Dorn assumed command. Conse-

[10] Walker to Davis, April 27, 1861, *Official Records,* Ser. IV, Vol. I, p. 250.

[11] Report of Committee, January 29, 1862, *ibid.,* pp. 885–886.

[12] Several payrolls are in Birge Papers, Case 12.

[13] *Ibid.*

[14] Harry N. Scheiber, "The Pay of the Troops and Confederate Morale in the Trans-Mississippi West," *Arkansas Historical Quarterly,* XVIII (Winter, 1959), 3.

[15] Holmes to Randolph, September 8, and October 2, 5, 1862, *Official Records,* Ser. I, Vol. XIII, pp. 877–878, 897.

quently, quartermaster general Myers relieved Adams and in July ordered Major Charles E. Carr, who had served in supply at Norfolk, Virginia, to join Holmes at Little Rock as chief quartermaster of the whole Trans-Mississippi Department.[16]

Although Myers continued to regard Carr as chief quartermaster of the Department, Adams continued to serve in that capacity until mid-December, when he retired from the service. Holmes then chose Major W. L. Cabell, who had distinguished himself at First Manassas, as already noted.[17] Carr was named by Holmes to direct the "Pay Department." Carr's position would be fixed finally by Kirby-Smith the following spring when he confirmed Carr as his chief paymaster.[18]

Carr arrived in Little Rock with $4 million in treasury notes, which he soon exhausted in bringing Arkansas payrolls up to April 30 or August 31, 1862, in paying for supplies, and in forwarding $1 million to General Taylor in Louisiana. After this, during the months of Holmes' regime, Carr seems to have confined his attentions mainly to Arkansas; Taylor and Magruder, in Texas, were directed to apply directly to Richmond for funds. Here, then, may have been a step backward in organization; decentralization of effort was a complaint against Holmes which the subsequent appointment of Kirby-Smith was designed to correct.

Declaring himself incapable of coping with the array of debt against the government, Carr sought to subordinate it to the immediate needs for supplies and payroll.[19]

Some of Carr's funds may have come into N. A. Birge's hands for disposition. Birge's papers show that he was often custodian for large sums of quartermaster money after he was transferred to Post Monroe in the fall of 1862. On November 2, 1862, he turned over $367,057.30 of Pay Bureau funds to the chief quartermaster of the

[16] The writer is indebted to Professor Harry N. Scheiber for notes on Carr's background. Scheiber, "Pay of the Troops and Confederate Morale," *Arkansas Historical Quarterly,* XVIII (Winter, 1959), 3.

[17] Announcement in *Arkansas Patriot,* December 18, 1862.

[18] *Ibid.*

[19] *Ibid.,* p. 5; Charles E. Carr Letterbooks. This important set of manuscripts, consisting of four letterbooks, cover Carr's operations from June 1861 to May 1865. Hereafter referred to as Carr Letterbooks.

North Louisiana Military District,[20] and his monthly statement for December, 1862, shows $385,969.20 transferred to the Pay Bureau.[21] Funds, then, were available for the payrolls in the winter of 1862 in the Monroe area.

The Pay Bureau, 1863–1865

Finding himself without funds at the end of 1862, Major Carr decided to go personally to Richmond to obtain a supply.[22] While in Richmond he learned of the decision to centralize the Trans-Mississippi under the highly regarded Kirby-Smith. Smith, by a General Order of June 15, 1863, endorsed Carr for continued service as chief of the Pay Bureau.[23] The office would now operate as another sub-bureau companion of the Clothing Bureau, the Tax-in-Kind Bureau, the Cotton Bureau, the Field Transportation Bureau—like them, operating under Lieutenant Colonel L. W. O'Bannon's main Quartermaster Bureau at Marshall, Texas.

After several months' absence in Richmond, Carr returned to his place in the Pay Bureau. He brought with him, or acquired in the Trans-Mississippi Department, funds sufficient to pay nearly all troops through April 30, 1863. Carr required all quartermasters to report fully to him so that he could direct redistribution of funds when he detected a surplus.

Despite all efforts, however, the fall of 1863 found the Bureau again without currency. Funds did not come until November—the point of desperation throughout the Department. Troops were promptly handed four months' pay, which Carr believed paid them all up to August 31, 1863.[24] In June, 1864, Carr had to report that

[20] Receipt, Birge Papers, Case 12.

[21] *Ibid.*, Case 13.

[22] Some troops were paid in Arkansas in February, 1863. Edward W. Cade, surgeon in Randal's Regiment, wrote his wife on February 7 that he would receive two months' pay in a few days. John Q. Anderson, *A Texas Surgeon in the C.S.A.* (Confederate Centennial Studies No. 6), p. 35.

[23] General Orders No. 19, June 15, 1863, *General Orders, Trans-Mississippi Department*, p. 13.

[24] Scheiber finds evidence that Carr erred in this assumption, as "several units in western Louisiana were not paid to that date for several months" more. "Pay of the Troops and Confederate Morale," *Arkansas Historical Quarterly*, XVIII (Winter, 1959), 10. Inclosure O, Carr to J. P. Johnson, January 19, 1864, *Official Records*, Ser. I, Vol. XXII, Pt. II, p. 1137.

no additional pay had been delivered. Study of Carr's letterbooks provides the conclusion that many Trans-Mississippi units were never paid beyond October, 1863.[25] Some funds arrived in May, 1864, but O'Bannon and Carr recognized that it would be an injustice to the troops to make a payroll anywhere until a new issue of treasury notes became available. Troops paid in the old notes would have found themselves subject to a 33⅓-per-cent tax on July 1.[26] Despite official hope that troop morale might be improved by this consideration, many must have been unhappy at being without pay for nearly a year.

After being paid, the men found that their money was almost worthless, as prices continued to rise and currency to decline in value. In March, 1861, the Confederate Congress fixed a private's pay at $11.00, and this pittance was not increased until June 9, 1864, when the magnificent sum of $18.00 per month was authorized. The civil workers in the government managed to get their salaries doubled in January, 1864, but even this was said to be only "a very slight concession to their needs, in view of the enormous inflation of the price of necessaries." Without doubt, the soldier's pay did not purchase much of anything in the inflationary chaos which characterized the whole economy of the Confederacy.[27]

Financial Collapse

In the fall and winter of 1864, the Trans-Mississippi Department grew increasingly desperate for money to meet its obligations. General Smith appealed on February 11 to P. W. Gray, chief of the Treasury's Trans-Mississippi branch, asking if something could not be done. Gray replied realistically, "I am fully aware of an alarming

[25] Carr to D. F. Shall, departmental auditor, April 3, 1865, Carr Letterbooks.

[26] Carr to district paymasters, May 13, 1864, *ibid.;* Carr to Smith, June 10, 1864, *Official Records,* Ser. I, Vol. XXIV, Pt. IV, p. 659. The congressional act of February 19, 1864, aimed to reduce the currency by taxing the notes out of circulation and forcing their exchange for bonds. The July 1 deadline for funding without penalty applied to notes of denominations above $5.00 and under $100.00. Notes of small denomination were not taxable until October 1 in the Trans-Mississippi. See John Christian Schwab, *The Confederate States of America, 1861–1865: A Financial and Industrial History of the South During the Civil War,* pp. 64–65; and Todd, *Confederate Finance,* pp. 112–113.

[27] Schwab, *Confederate States of America,* pp. 166–174.

and calamitous condition. It is faithfully described by you, and must soon overwhelm us, unless the Government provides relief . . ." The Secretary of the Treasury had been fully informed of the Department's difficulties, Gray reported, and a special messenger had been sent to Richmond to bring back such funds as he could pry from the main source; but the government had none for him. Gray gloomily concluded his reply to Smith as follows: "I have still hope that the Government couriers, Messrs Ewell & Co. will shortly arrive with some addition to our funds, but must say that I do not expect a sufficient amount of them to meet even for a short time, the military necessities of the Department." [28]

Although Gray had Treasury couriers in the east to obtain funds, Smith decided to send his own messengers. Paymaster Carr told correspondents in early April that the General had sent two officers by different routes to Richmond bearing estimates "of all arrearages due in this Dep't." Pay Bureau share of the arrearages now totalled in excess of $60 million.[29] Nothing would come of that Richmond journey; Grant was already moving into possession of the city. Carr, however, remained on duty and faithfully kept up his official journal until May 15, 1865. An ironic commentary on the devotion of the quartermaster to his procedural system is provided by the last item in the book—a formal note acknowledging receipt of a return from the paymaster of the West Louisiana District. Carr most certainly must have forwarded it to O'Bannon's bureau at Marshall for final audit!

Financial collapse was now complete, and even the expensive barter system involving massive cotton deliveries to the Rio Grande could not remedy the situation. Money was a necessity, and the increasing lack of it had been one of the principal obstacles to the quartermaster from the beginning of the war. Major Haynes of the Clothing Bureau was greatly handicapped by official poverty, as were all of the post quartermaster officers of the Tax-in-Kind Bureau, the Cotton Bureau, the Field Transportation Bureau, and the

[28] Gray to Smith, February 24, 1865, Kirby-Smith Papers.
[29] Carr to J. H. Beck, April 4, 1865, and Carr to Thompson Harrison, April 7, 1865, Carr Letterbooks.

Pay Bureau. Professor Schwab has stated that the Confederate financial policy ranks with the Federal blockade as the agencies which most weakened Southern resistance. Kirby-Smith's biographer, Professor Joseph Parks, found that financial demoralization was more disastrous to the Trans-Mississippi Department than were military reverses.[30] The government, at Secretary Memminger's instigation, early committed itself to a paper-money policy, neglected taxation, and continued to rely on increasing quantities of noninterest-bearing notes to pay its domestic debts.[31] In the words of Schwab, "The verdict passed upon the cause of the Confederate States will not emphasize the mistaken financial policy adopted by the Government, but rather the fact that in spite of it, the South maintained herself so long." [32] Quartermaster officers of the Trans-Mississippi undoubtedly would have echoed those words. As Frank Vandiver phrased it, "The stark fact about money which most concerned supply officers was that it was scarce and grew scarcer and less valuable as the war progressed." [33] The most recent student of Confederate finance, Professor Todd, while making no effort to gloss over the inadequacies of the Confederate money effort, points out what may seem obvious but needs to be said: "The decisive agent . . . in determining the stability or soundness of Confederate finance rested in the success or failure of the military. It was upon the failure of the armed forces to achieve their goal that Confederate finance collapsed." [34] Quartermaster officers of the Trans-Mississippi would no doubt have echoed this opinion, if "failure of the military" were construed so as to imply no lack of intelligent and honest effort.

[30] Parks, *General Edmund Kirby Smith,* p. 448.
[31] Schwab, *Confederate States of America,* pp. 18, 69, 70, 312.
[32] *Ibid.,* p. 312.
[33] Vandiver, *Rebel Brass,* pp. 88–89.
[34] Todd, *Confederate Finance,* p. 156.

VII

A Resumé of Difficulties

The Trans-Mississippi area lacked a centralized, coordinated command until July, 1862, and this factor adversely affected quartermaster operations in the first two years of the war. The western states began the war with only the military supplies seized in the first months from United States Army forces stationed within their borders. Mobilizing units therefore equipped themselves with the help of their home communities. The states of Texas, Arkansas, and Louisiana organized and supplied regiments of troops, which were soon transferred to Confederate service.

Comparatively few quartermaster officers were assigned to supply operations in the Trans-Mississippi in the first year of the war, and Confederate equipment came principally from civilian contributions, which were donated or sold either to the state governments or to the unit quartermasters.

Quartermasters of organizations were responsible for all of the duties listed in the *Army Regulations* for their departments. With no network or system of supply depots to draw from, they purchased locally and appealed to the people until some system could be established. When a system did develop, it took a bureaucratic form, with the Quartermaster's Department breaking up into sub-bureaus responsible for various functions.

Although the Quartermaster's Department never completely freed itself from the need of recourse to popular donations, it established a

Clothing Bureau in 1862, after the Trans-Mississippi Department had been created. Thereafter, all officers and agents working at clothing supply followed the policies and program of the chief of the Bureau, and their efforts provided a significant quantity of badly needed supplies. If the war had continued, indications are that the Bureau might have made the Trans-Mississippi Department self-sufficient as to clothing supply. Several factors handicapped and delayed satisfactory results in 1863 and 1864: the failure of ac-credited purchasing agents to fill requisitions, the loss of Browns-ville, the fall of Vicksburg and the interruption of intercourse with the east, and the depreciation of the currency. Bureau hopes picked up again after the recovery of Brownsville and the acceleration of the Matamoros traffic in late 1864.

Another quartermaster bureau appeared in 1864 as a result of the passage of a tax-in-kind act by the Confederate Congress. The act required that one-tenth of the crops of 1863 be delivered to the government. A system of post quartermasters (one to each congres-sional district), operating under state quartermasters, and super-vised by the assistant quartermaster general, collected the tithe. In 1864 a bureau was established in the Trans-Mississippi Department to direct and coordinate state controlling officers and post quarter-masters in the extensive collection system. The tithe accomplished its purpose in the Trans-Mississippi in that immense quantities of commissary supplies were obtained, thus alleviating the food prob-lem of the commissary service. In 1864 a second tithe act was passed by Congress and the collection and accounting for it by quartermasters continued until the end of the war. Chief difficulties experienced by the Tax-in-Kind (tithe) Bureau were conscription of its numerous civilian employees (depot agents, teamsters, etc.), depreciation of the currency, and shortage of transportation.

The shortage of transportation experienced by the tax-in-kind officers was partly a consequence of the operations of the Cotton Bureau. This office, established by General Kirby-Smith in the au-tumn of 1863, sought to obtain a maximum of cotton from the planters in order that it might be hauled to the Rio Grande in ox-drawn wagons and exchanged for munitions and supplies from

Europe and Mexico. Confederate officers had great hopes for the plan, and it did provide a great quantity of essential supplies, but again certain factors impeded operations. Speculation by private individuals, the competition of Texas state authorities, and currency problems were the principal obstacles encountered by the Cotton Bureau. Both speculators and state agents offered better terms to the planter than the Confederate officer could afford. Drastic action was taken late in 1864 to eliminate this competition, but it was too late for a satisfactory exploitation of cotton exchange.

Although both the Cotton Bureau and the Tax-in-Kind Bureau often suffered for want of transportation equipment, the armies in the field in the Trans-Mississippi were generally adequately supplied with such equipment during the last two years of the war. This favorable situation derived from the efforts of a specialized unit of quartermaster officers constituting the Field Transportation Bureau and from the fortunes of the battlefield. In the retreat of General Banks' Federal forces after the Battles of Mansfield and Pleasant Hill in the spring of 1864, and in the battles around Camden, Arkansas, and in numerous lesser encounters, the Confederates captured much transportation equipment. Supervising (after January, 1864), the supply, repair, and inspection of all field transportation was the Field Transportation Bureau, which operated under the Quartermaster's Department. By the latter part of 1864 efforts of the new Bureau enabled its chief to report adequate transportation on hand for the armies in the field and to be optimistic about the future. Several serious difficulties, however, constantly harassed officers. Shortage of horses, lack of iron, and a lack of sufficient funds were chief worries. Texas had recruited numerous cavalry units, causing a shortage of horses for transportation purposes; the iron problem was one of industrial resources; and the monetary difficulty was a general problem that seriously handicapped all quartermasters, as is detailed in preceding paragraphs.[1]

[1] An attempt to explain the causes of the failure of Confederate finances has been the subject of able monographs by Professors Smith and Schwab and, more recently, by Professor Todd. See Ernest Ashton Smith, *The History of the Confederate Treasury*, p. 1901; Schwab, *The Confederate States of America;* Todd, *Confederate Finance.*

Inasmuch as depreciation of the currency generally obstructed efforts of all the quartermaster agencies discussed above, some attention must be given the problem in the present study. The evidence reveals that the paper-money policy followed by the Confederate government failed to establish a sound currency. Inflation occurred, the people were loathe to sell their goods for the depreciating paper, and the quartermaster's funds, even when he had them, failed to procure nearly what he had hoped they would provide.

A quartermaster bureau closely concerned with the currency problem was the Pay Bureau. Operating under a Trans-Mississippi Department paymaster, District paymasters distributed funds to the regimental quartermasters who did the actual paying of the troops. The task was handled capably by the responsible officers, but the mere delivery of his pittance to a soldier did not give the money any buying power.

Confronted constantly with money troubles and the other problems summarized above and discussed in the foregoing chapters, the Trans-Mississippi quartermaster operated under almost hopeless circumstances. Had the Confederate authorities in Richmond early recognized the potential importance of Matamoros as a port and provided the military in the Trans-Mississippi with the power to commandeer cotton resources available west of the river, there would probably have been a surfeit of everything in the way of military supplies for the Department. Eventual recognition of the need for coordinated control of international trade brought greatly improved marketing conditions to the whole Confederacy late in 1864, but by then Sherman was on his way to Savannah. Given more time in the Trans-Mississippi, the quartermaster might have realized some of his dreams. As it was, in spite of its difficulties, this organization of officers managed to maintain its forces in the field for four long years.

Bibliography

PRIMARY SOURCES

Manuscripts

Birge (Captain N. A.) Papers. 1861–1865. These quartermaster papers constitute a large part of the "General Papers of the Period of the Confederacy" (Heartman Collection) in the Archives of the Library of the University of Texas, Austin, Texas. The documents, consisting of 3,173 pieces, together with seven ledger books, were the wartime papers of Captain N. A. Birge, assistant quartermaster, Confederate States Army, who served in the Trans-Mississippi throughout the war. The papers include every type of requisition, bill, receipt, report, account, and official paper used by the Confederate Quartermaster's Department and are a particularly valuable source for study of the Cotton Bureau's operations.

Blake (Bennett) Papers. Several items illustrating Confederate tax forms may be found in this set of manuscripts in the East Texas Collection, Library of Stephen F. Austin State College, Nacogdoches, Texas.

Botts (Benjamin A.) Correspondence Journal, or Letterbook, styled "Texas Controlling Quartermaster." This journal is in the Archives of The University of Texas Library, Austin, Texas. Major Botts, who directed the collection of the tax-in-kind in the Trans-Mississippi Department, used this ledger to record file copies of his outgoing letters. Since the letters were so worded as to indicate also the content of much of the incoming mail, the journal is even more valuable as a source for a study of the tithe acts in operation.

Cabell (W. L.) Papers. Two items. The originals are the property of Mr. Earle Cabell of Dallas, Texas. Other Cabell items are among the collections of the Dallas Historical Museum, Dallas, Texas.

Carr (Charles E.) Letterbooks. These four volumes cover Carr's operations from June, 1861, to May, 1865. They are in the collections of the New York Historical Society, New York.

Confederate States Army Collection (I), 1860–1865. Department of Archives and Manuscripts, Louisiana State University Library, Baton Rouge, Louisiana.

Fogle (Andrew J.) Papers. Twenty-eight letters. Archives of the Library of The University of Texas, Austin, Texas.

Hardin (J. Fair) Collection. Department of Archives and Manuscripts, Louisiana State University Library, Baton Rouge, Louisiana.

Hill (G. H.) Letterbook, styled "Letters Sent by Lt. Col. G. H. Hill, Commander of the Confederate Ordnance Works at Tyler, Texas, 1864–1865." The National Archives, Washington, D.C., lists this item as Volume 147, Chapter IV, Record Group 109. Microfilm copy in possession of writer.

Kirby-Smith (Edmund) Papers. Southern Historical Collection, University of North Carolina, Chapel Hill, North Carolina. Copy in Ramsdell microfilms, Roll 209–B, Archives of The University of Texas Library, Austin, Texas. Only a few documents in this collection bear directly on quartermaster affairs.

Miscellaneous Records of the Quartermaster and Commissary Departments for the State of Texas and the Confederate States, 1861–1865. The Archives of the State of Texas contain a mass of quartermaster manuscript materials assembled in portfolios which also contain various commissary papers. State and Confederate quartermaster papers are intermingled, but the records and papers of Captain George C. Rives, post quartermaster for the Sixth Congressional District of Texas, seem quite complete and fully illustrate details of the tax-in-kind collection. The various portfolios bear different labels, and are cited individually in this study.

Quartermaster-General Letterbooks, Volumes 199 and 199½. These volumes are in Chapter V, Record Group 109, The National Archives, Washington, D.C.

Rives (George C.) Correspondence. Miscellaneous Records of the Quartermaster and Commissary Departments for the State of Texas and the Confederate States, 1861–1865, Archives of Texas State Library, Austin, Texas.

Roberts (Mrs. William) Paper. A letter to her niece, dated November 24, 1861. The original is in the possession of Mrs. James W. Stevenson, Victoria, Texas. Mrs. Roberts was the great-great-grandmother of the present writer.

Sims (J. W.) Letterbook. Sims was post quartermaster at Natchitoches, Louisiana. His letterbook is included in the J. Fair Hardin Collection, Department of Archives and Manuscripts, Louisiana State University Library, Baton Rouge, Louisiana.

Smith, Edmund Kirby. See Kirby-Smith.

Texas Cotton Bureau Letterbook. This important volume, containing the letters sent from 1863 to 1865 by Hutchins, Broadwell, and Wells, is listed as Vol. 46 in Record Group 56, National Archives, Washington, D.C.

Wise (James Calvert) Papers. Russell Library, Northwestern State College, Natchitoches, Louisiana. Approximately 1,000 items. Wise was chief quartermaster for the state of Louisiana. The papers primarily reflect activities of several Louisiana officials in the general supply of state troops. Several items bear on Confederate quartermaster operations.

Printed Material

Government Publications

Army Regulations Adopted for the Use of the Army of the Confederate States. Richmond, Virginia: West & Johnston, Publishers, 1861.

Bloomfield, B. *The Quartermaster's Guide, Being a Compilation From the Army Regulations and Other Sources: Also the Pay Bureau of the Quartermaster's Department.* Houston, Texas: R. W. Cave, Publisher, 1863.

"Cotton Sold to the Confederate States." *United States Senate Document No. 987,* 62nd Congress, 3rd Session. Washington, D.C.: Government Printing Office, 1913.

General Orders from the Adjutant and Inspector-General's Office, Confederate States Army, From January 1, 1864, to July 1, 1864, Inclusive. Columbia, South Carolina: Evans and Cogswell, Printers, 1864.

General Orders, Headquarters, Trans-Mississippi Department, From March 6, 1863, to January 1, 1865. Published by authority. Houston, Texas: E. H. Cushing & Co., 1865.

Journal of Both Sessions of the Convention of the State of Arkansas. Published by authority. Little Rock, Arkansas, 1861.

Lester, W. W., and W. J. Bromwell (eds.). *A Digest of the Military and Naval Laws of the Confederate States, From the Commencement of the Provisional Congress to the End of the First Congress under the Permanent Constitution.* Columbia, South Carolina: Evans and Cogswell, Printers, 1864.

Matthews, James M. (ed.). *The Statutes at Large of the Provisional Government of the Confederate States of America* . . . Richmond, Virginia: R. M. Smith, Printer, 1864.

Record Group 56. Volume 46. National Archives, Washington, D.C.

Record Group 109. Chapter IV, Volume 147; Chapter V, Volume 199; Chapter V, Volume 199½. National Archives, Washington, D.C.

Regulations of the Army of the Confederate States, 1862, Containing a Complete Set of Forms. Austin, Texas: Printed at *State Gazette* office, 1862.

Regulations of the Confederate States Army for the Quartermaster's Department, Including the Pay Branch Thereof. Richmond, Virginia: J. W. Randolph, 1864.

Senate Document No. 987, 62nd Congress, 3rd Session. The full title of this document reads: "Statement B (Texas): List of persons who sold cotton to the Confederate States through the Texas Cotton Bureau, located at Houston, Texas, and operated under direction of the Confederate Military Department of the Trans-Mississippi." Washington, D.C.: Government Printing Office, 1913.

The War of the Rebellion: A Compilation of the Official Records of the Union and Confederate Armies. 70 volumes in 128; United States government publication arranged in four series. Washington, D.C., 1880–1901.

Contemporary Accounts and Reminiscences

Anderson, John Q. (ed.). *Brokenburn, The Journal of Kate Stone, 1861–1868.* Baton Rouge, Louisiana: Louisiana State University Press, 1955.

Fremantle, Arthur James Lyon. *The Fremantle Diary: Being the Journal of Lieutenant Colonel James Arthur Lyon Fremantle, Coldstream Guards, on His Three Months in the Southern States.* Edited by Walter Lord. Boston: Little, Brown & Company, 1954.

Gammage, W. L. *The Camp, the Bivouac, and the Battle Field.* Selma, Alabama: C.S.A. publication, 1864. Reprinted in Little Rock, Arkansas: Arkansas Southern Press, 1958.

Heartsill, William W. *Fourteen Hundred and 91 Days, in the Confederate Army: A Journal Kept by (above) for Four Years, One Month, and One Day, Or Camp Life, Day-By-Day, of the W. P. Lane Rangers, From April 19, 1861, to May 20, 1865.* Marshall, Texas: Printed by the author, 1876.

Yeary, Mamie (comp.). *Reminiscences of the Boys in Gray, 1861–1865.* Dallas, Texas: Privately printed, 1912. Facsimile reprint, Ed. Bell I. Wiley. Jackson, Tennessee: McCowat-Mercer Press, 1954.

Newspapers

Arkansas Patriot (Little Rock), January, 1862–September 1, 1863. In the Newspaper Collection of The University of Texas Library, Austin.

Bellville Countryman (Bellville, Texas), August 21, 1861–June 1, 1865. In the Newspaper Collection of The University of Texas Library, Austin.

Daily State Journal (Little Rock), November 1, 1861–February 7, 1862. In the Newspaper Collection of The University of Texas Library, Austin.

Dallas Herald, July 17, 1861–February 23, 1865. In the Newspaper Collection of The University of Texas Library, Austin.

Galveston Tri-Weekly News. Copies dated July 15, 1862–February, 1862, and January, 1864–May, 1865, in the Newspaper Collection of The University of Texas Library, Austin. Copies dated April, 1862–January, 1865, in Texas State Library, Austin.

News Messenger (Marshall, Texas), November 26, 1961. Personal copy of author.

Patriot (La Grange, Texas). Copies dated June, 1863–June, 1865, in Texas State Library, Austin. Copies dated January, 1865–July, 1865, in Newspaper Collection of The University of Texas Library, Austin.

Semi-Weekly Citizen (Des Arc, Arkansas), August, 1861–December, 1861. In possession of Arkansas History Commission, Little Rock. Microfilm copies in University of Arkansas Library, Fayetteville.

Southwestern (Shreveport, Louisiana), April, 1863–May, 1865. In the Newspaper Collection of The University of Texas Library, Austin.

Texas Almanac—Extra (Austin), November 1, 1862–June, 1863. In the Newspaper Collection of The University of Texas Library, Austin.

Washington Telegraph (Arkansas), January 15, 1862–December, 1865. In possession of Arkansas History Commission, Little Rock. Microfilm copies in University of Arkansas Library, Fayetteville.

SECONDARY SOURCES

Books

Anderson, John Q. *A Texas Surgeon in the C.S.A.* Confederate Centennial Studies No. 6. Tuscaloosa, Alabama: Confederate Publishing Company, Inc., 1957.

Black, Robert C., III. *The Railroads of the Confederacy.* Chapel Hill, North Carolina: University of North Carolina Press, 1952.

Bragg, Jefferson Davis. *Louisiana in the Confederacy.* Baton Rouge, Louisiana: Louisiana State University Press, 1941.

Brooks, Robert Preston. "Alexander R. Lawton," in *Dictionary of American Biography* (edited by Allen Johnson and Dumas Malone). 21 vols. New York: Charles Scribner's Sons, 1928–1944.

Coulter, E. Merton. *The Confederate States of America, 1861–1865.* Baton Rouge, Louisiana: Louisiana State University Press, 1950.

Cunningham, Frank. *General Stand Watie's Confederate Indians.* San Antonio, Texas: Naylor Press, 1959.

Davis, Charles S. *Colin J. McRae: Confederate Financial Agent.* Confederate Centennial Studies No. 17. Tuscaloosa, Alabama: Confederate Publishing Company, Inc., 1961.

Evans, Clement A. (ed.). *Confederate Military History, a Library of Confederate History.* 12 vols. Atlanta, Georgia: Confederate Publishing Company, 1899.

Freeman, Douglas Southall. *The South to Posterity.* New York: Charles Scribner's Sons, 1939.

Hall, Martin Hardwick. *Sibley's New Mexico Campaign.* Austin, Texas: University of Texas Press, 1960.

Johnson, Ludwell H. *Red River Campaign: Politics and Cotton in the Civil War.* Baltimore: Johns Hopkins Press, 1958.

Lea, Tom. *The King Ranch.* 2 vols. Boston: Little, Brown & Company, 1957.

Lonn, Ella. *Salt As a Factor in the Confederacy.* New York: W. Neale, 1933.

Owsley, Frank L. *King Cotton Diplomacy: Foreign Relations of the Confederate States of America.* Chicago: University of Chicago Press, 1931.

Parks, Joseph Howard. *General Edmund Kirby Smith, C.S.A.* Baton Rouge, Louisiana: Louisiana State University Press, 1954.

Potts, Charles S. *Railroad Transportation in Texas.* Bulletin No. 119 of The University of Texas, Austin, Texas, 1909.

Ramsdell, Charles W. "Abraham Charles Myers," in *Dictionary of American Biography* (edited by Allen Johnson and Dumas Malone). 21 vols. New York: Charles Scribner's Sons, 1928–1944.

————. *Behind the Lines of the Southern Confederacy.* Baton Rouge, Louisiana: Louisiana State University Press, 1944.

Reed, S. G. *A History of the Texas Railroads and of Transportation Conditions Under Spain and Mexico and the Republic and the State.* Houston, Texas: St. Clair Publishing Co., 1941.

Schwab, John Christian. *The Confederate States of America, 1861–1865: A Financial and Industrial History of the South During the Civil War.* New Haven, Connecticut: Yale University Press, 1901.

Smith, Ernest Ashton. *The History of the Confederate Treasury.* Harrisburg, Pennsylvania: Harrisburg Publishing Company, 1901.

Taylor, George Rogers, and Irene D. Neu. *The American Railroad Network, 1861–1890.* Cambridge, Massachusetts: Harvard University Press, 1956.

Thomas, David Y. *Arkansas in War and Reconstruction, 1861–1874.* Little Rock, Arkansas: Arkansas Division, United Daughters of the Confederacy, 1926.

Thompson, Samuel Bernard. *Confederate Purchasing Operations Abroad.* Chapel Hill, North Carolina: University of North Carolina Press, 1935.

Todd, Richard Cecil. *Confederate Finance.* Athens, Georgia: University of Georgia Press, 1954.

Vandiver, Frank E. (ed.). *Confederate Blockade Running Through Bermuda 1861–1865: Letters and Cargo Manifests.* Austin, Texas: University of Texas Press, 1947.

Vandiver, Frank E. *Rebel Brass, The Confederate Command System.* Baton Rouge, Louisiana: Louisiana State University Press, 1956.

Weigley, Russell F. *Quartermaster General of the Union Army: A Biography of M. C. Meigs.* New York: Columbia University Press, 1959.

Wiley, Bell I. *The Life of Johnny Reb*. New York: Bobbs-Merrill Company, Inc., 1943.

Articles

Barr, Alwyn. "Texas Coastal Defense, 1861–1865," *Southwestern Historical Quarterly*, XLV (July, 1961), 1–31.

Cabell, W. L. "True History of Our Battle Flag," *Confederate Veteran*, XI (August, 1903), 1.

Delaney, Robert W. "Matamoros, Port for Texas during the Civil War," *Southwestern Historical Quarterly*, LVIII (April, 1955), 473–487.

Diamond, William. "Imports of the Confederate Government from Europe and Mexico," *Journal of Southern History*, VI (November, 1940), 470–503.

Holladay, Florence E. "The Powers of the Commander of the Confederate Trans-Mississippi Department, 1863–1865," *Southwestern Historical Quarterly*, XXI (1918), 279–298; 333–359.

Nichols, James L. "Confederate Engineer Odd Jobs," *The Military Engineer*, LIII (January–February, 1961), 13–15.

————. "The Tax-in-Kind in the Department of the Trans-Mississippi," *Civil War History*, V (December, 1959), 382–389.

————. "The Operations of Captain N. A. Birge, Confederate Quartermaster at Monroe, Louisiana, 1862–1863," *Louisiana Studies*, I (Fall, 1962), 23–29.

Ramsdell, Charles W. "Some Problems Involved in Writing the History of the Confederacy," *Journal of Southern History*, II (May, 1936), 133–147.

————. "The Confederate Government and the Railroads," *American Historical Review*, XXII (July, 1917), 794–810.

————. "The Control of Manufacturing by the Confederate Government," *Mississippi Valley Historical Review*, VIII (December, 1921), 231–249.

————. "The Texas State Military Board, 1862–1865," *Southwestern Historical Quarterly*, XXVII (April, 1924), 253–275.

Rusling, J. F. "A Word for the Quartermaster's Department," *United States Service Magazine*, III (January, 1865), 57–67.

Scheiber, Harry N. "The Pay of the Troops and Confederate Morale in the Trans-Mississippi West," *Arkansas Historical Quarterly*, XVIII (Winter, 1959), 1–16.

Windham, William T. "The Problem of Supply in the Trans-Mississippi Confederacy," *Journal of Southern History*, XXVII (May, 1961), 149–168.

Unpublished Theses and Dissertations

Bramlette, John Edwin. "Railroad Development in Texas before 1861." Master of Arts thesis, The University of Texas, 1941.

Cowling, Annie. "The Civil War Trade of the Lower Rio Grande." Master of Arts thesis, The University of Texas, 1926.

Dufner, Lucille. "The Flags of the Confederate States of America." Master of Arts thesis, The University of Texas, 1944.

Ellsworth, Lois Council. "San Antonio During the Civil War." Master of Arts thesis, The University of Texas, 1938.

Felgar, Robert P. "Texas in the War for Southern Independence." Ph.D. dissertation, The University of Texas, 1935.

Goodlet, Margaret N. "The Enforcement of the Confederate Conscription Acts in the Trans-Mississippi Department." Master of Arts thesis, The University of Texas, 1914.

Lambie, Agnes L. "Confederate Control of Cotton in the Trans-Mississippi Department." Master of Arts thesis, The University of Texas, 1915.

Megee, Jonnie M. "The Confederate Impressment Acts in the Trans-Mississippi States." Master of Arts thesis, The University of Texas, 1915.

Index

Adams, John D.: as chief quartermaster, 5; corresponds with Birge, 13; on clothing manufacture, 29; relief of, 96; continues as chief quartermaster, 97; mentioned, 27 and 27 n.

Adelaide (ship): 66

Alexander Collie & Co.: purchases from, 66

Alexander Ross & Co.: purchases from, 66

Alexandria, Louisiana: purchasing offices in, 12; field transportation at, 89; mentioned, 29, 59

Allen, H. W. (Governor): cotton purchasing by, 62 n.

Alleyton, Texas: as cotton center, 55; cotton depot at, 69; mentioned, 72, 91

Anderson County, Texas: 64

Archer Grays: clothes for, 20

Arizona: as part of Texas District, 5

Arizona Battery: river transportation for, 10–11

Arkadelphia, Arkansas: as principal quartermaster post, 10; river traffic to, 10; wagon trains from, 11; mentioned, 12

Arkansas, District of: as division of Trans-Mississippi Department, 4; clothing supply in, 23 and n.; clothing for Texas troops in, 27; tax-in-kind collection in, 45; pay of troops in, 97, 98 n.; transportation in, 88, 89; mentioned, 30, 96

Arkansas Military Board: supply efforts of, 23

Arnold, James R.: as controlling quartermaster (tax-in-kind) for Texas, 46; mentioned, 50

Ashe, W. S.: superintends Confederate transportation, 83, 90

Austin, Texas: clothing depot at, 20; Ladies Aid Society of, 24; supply depot at, 25; shoe supply in, 34; as tax-in-kind collection center, 46; mentioned, 27, 48, 78 n., 84

Avery Island (Louisiana): production of salt at, 11

Bagdad, Mexico: village of, 57 n.; ships at, 82 n.

Ball, George: associates with Texas Cotton Bureau, 64

Banks, N. P.: loses wagon train, 87–88; equipment of, captured, 105; mentioned, 38–39, 55 n.

Barrett, W. W.: and Cotton Bureau, 63–65, 64 n., 68; mentioned, 59

Bayou City Guards: clothing for, 20

Bayou Teche (Louisiana): river traffic to, 10

Beaumont, Texas: clothing depot at, 20

Beauregard, Pierre G. T.: 13 n.

Bee, H. P.: well-dressed troops of, 38; competes with Major Hart, 53; cotton impressment by, 56, 57; mentioned, 55, 73

mentioned, 14, 29, 97
Hopkins County, Texas: 64 n.
Houston Artillery: clothing for, 20
Houston, Texas: as headquarters for "Military Department of Texas," 4; clothing depot at, 20; Ladies' Aid Society in, 20; Clothing Bureau depot in, 31, 33; shoe manufacture in, 34; as office of Cotton Bureau, 64; field transportation office in, 87; mentioned, 40–41, 80, 91
Houston Tri-Weekly Telegraph: on transportation officers, 89–90
Hunt County, Texas: 64 n.
Huntsville, Texas: 29, 34–35, 35 n.
Huse, Caleb: purchases from, 66
Hutchins, W. J.: heads Texas Cotton Bureau, 64; explains relation to Broadwell, 64; 1864 reports of, 69, 79–80; corresponds with planters, 71; and funds for Rio Grande troops, 73; mentioned, 66, 70, 73, 78, 87

impressment: by tax-in-kind officers, 50; Congress acts on, 75; of cotton, 62–63, 75; of wagons and horses, 75; resistance to, 76
Indianola, Texas: as headquarters for Van Dorn, 4
Indian Territory: as part of Arkansas District, 4; command problems in, 33; transportation in, 89
Indian troops: clothing shortages of, 32

Jackson County, Texas: tax-in-kind collection in, 48
Johnson, J. P.: inspects Trans-Mississippi Department, 34
Johnston, Joseph E.: 13 n.
Jefferson, Texas: clothing depot at, 19–20, 33; ladies' groups in, 21; quartermaster operations at, 22; Clothing Bureau agent in, 28–29; hat supply in, 34; mentioned, 63, 68

Kaufman County, Texas: holdups by women in, 68–69; mentioned, 64 n.
Keatchie, Louisiana: field transportation shop at, 89
M. Kenedy & Co.: Confederate contracts with, 57–58; Cotton Bureau contract with, 72 and n.

King, Richard: contract of, with Cotton Bureau, 72 and n.
Kirby-Smith, Edmund: commands Trans-Mississippi Department, 5, 30; and "Kirby-Smithdom," 5; allocates clothing, 33; quarrels with Taylor, 38–39; places Clothing Bureau under chief quartermaster, 40–41; on supply in Red River Campaign, 50–51; on cotton impressment, 50, 57, 75–76; establishes Cotton Bureau, 53, 58; on cotton frauds, 62; and Texas Cotton Bureau, 64; sends agent abroad, 65; sustains Cotton Bureau decision, 70–71; sets up Field Transportation Bureau, 83; continues Carr as paymaster, 98; appeals for financial help, 99–100; mentioned, 14, 43, 88, 90, 97, 100, 104
Kyle, W. J.: in Texas Cotton Bureau, 64

Lacey, J. Horace: heads Field Transportation Bureau, 87
Ladies' Aid Societies: supply by, 20–22, 24; in Louisiana, 23; appeal to, 31
Lafourche Creoles: clothing for, 23
Lafourche, Louisiana: Ladies' Volunteer Association of, 23
LaGrange, Texas: cotton depot at, 69
Lampasas County, Texas: 47
Lancaster, Texas: Ladies' Aid Society of, 21
Lark (steamer): 66
Lauve & Belknap: as treasury agents, 59
Lawton, A. R.: as quartermaster general, 4; on tithe collections, 47
Lemore & Co.: 59
Little Rock, Arkansas: as headquarters of Trans-Mississippi Department, 4; as quartermaster post, 10; purchasing offices in, 12; as Clothing Bureau headquarters, 30; mentioned, 29, 30
Lochalva (brig): 66
London, England: shipments from, 55–57
Louisiana, District of: as division of Trans-Mississippi Department, 5; ladies' sewing groups in, 23; clothing in, 24; transportation in, 89; quartermaster funds in, 98, 100
Louisiana, state of: quartermaster department of, 62 n.; mentioned, 102
Louisiana State Bank: cotton assets of, 61